THE MIND UP CURRICULUM

Grades 6–8

Focused Classrooms • Mindful Learning • Resilient Students

■SCHOLASTIC

Acknowledgments

With heartfelt appreciation to Goldie Hawn, Founder of The Hawn Foundation, for her vision, commitment, compassion, and dedicated advocacy for children everywhere.

We would like to thank the many scientists, researchers, and educators who contributed to the MindUP curriculum.

Pat Achtyl; Thelma Anselmi; Angie Balius; Lorraine Bayne; Michelle Beaulieu; Peter Canoll, MD, PhD; Beck Collie; Adele Diamond, PhD; Diane Dillon, PhD; Jennifer Erickson; Nancy Etcoff, PhD; Pam Hoeffner; Nicole Iorio; Greg Jabaut; Ann Kelly; Molly Stewart Lawlor; Noreen Maguire; Marc A. Meyer, PhD; Cindy Middendorf; Christine Boardman Moen; Tammy Murphy, PhD; Charlene Myklebust, PhD; Nicole Obadia; Carol B. Olson, PhD; Janice Parry; Lisa Pedrini; Tina Posner; Kimberly Schonert-Reichl, PhD; Patti Vitale; Judy Willis, MD, MEd; Victoria Zelenak

MINDUP
Table of Contents

Welcome to
MINDUP

Imagine … joyful learning, academic success, and a powerful sense of self and community.

Imagine … students who are able to engage in a focused, energetic way with one another, with their teachers, and with their learning.

Imagine … schools that are productive, harmonious centers of successful learning, where all students thrive because they recognize themselves as

- capable, creative learners
- self-aware human beings
- compassionate, responsible citizens

All of this is possible. **MINDUP** can help you achieve it.

MindUP Online Training

At **www.thehawnfoundation.org**, you'll find resources to enrich your MindUP instruction, including
- the entire spectrum of MindUP techniques, addressing social and emotional learning
- classroom demonstrations conducted by experienced MindUP consultants and mentors
- instructional insights, grade-specific teaching strategies, and other resources
- the latest in neuroscience about how the brain works and how it affects learning

Register at **www.thehawnfoundation.org** to access this innovative, interactive training and learning resource, developed in partnership with Columbia University's Center for New Media Teaching and Learning.

Dear Educators,

From Scholastic

For 90 years, Scholastic has been a presence in your classrooms, supporting teaching and learning. The challenges faced by you and your students today are well known and unprecedented. These include the following expectations:

- providing differentiated instruction to students who come with diverse language and experiential backgrounds
- improving academic performance
- addressing new standards geared to career and college preparedness
- helping your students and their families handle economic and social changes

When we met Goldie Hawn and the Hawn Foundation team, we were impressed by their commitment to helping all students achieve their potential socially and academically. Also, we shared their respect for educators who, like all of you, are entrusted with the preparation of the next generation.

We are pleased to introduce MindUP, a collaboration of the Hawn Foundation and Scholastic. MindUP isn't one more program to implement or subject to teach, but a set of strategies that can be integrated with what you are already doing, so that you and your students will become more focused when doing schoolwork and are able to work and play more successfully with others. The essence of what the MindUP program calls for is embodied in the idea of the Optimistic Classroom—a place where all children have the opportunity to achieve their potential.

Thank you for inviting us into your school.

Optimistically yours,

Francie Alexander   *Patrick Daley*

Francie Alexander
Chief Academic Officer
Scholastic Inc.

Patrick Daley
Senior Vice President, Publisher
Scholastic Inc.

From the Hawn Foundation

Thank you for bringing the MindUP Curriculum into your classrooms.

MindUP has been my focus and my passion for many years. I am so grateful to you, devoted educators who believe in the limitless potential of children and give tirelessly of your time, energy, creativity, and love.

The simple practices at the core of MindUP will help your students to become resilient, focused, and mindful learners. I have seen the MindUP practices at work in classrooms all over the world. I have witnessed its success and have heard from countless teachers in praise of its transformative effect on students' ability to learn.

I know that with your help we can equip our students with the skills they need to live smarter, healthier, and happier lives. Together we will create optimistic classrooms where students successfully cope with the stresses they face in school, at home, and in their communities.

Thank you for accepting the enormous and critically important responsibilities and challenges that accompany your mission as an educator.

From the bottom of my heart, I thank you.

Goldie Hawn

Goldie Hawn
Founder, The Hawn Foundation
and the MindUP Curriculum

What Is MindUP?

MindUP is a comprehensive, classroom-tested, evidence-based curriculum framed around 15 easily implemented lessons that foster social and emotional awareness, enhance psychological well-being, and promote academic success.

The MindUP classroom is an optimistic classroom that promotes and develops mindful attention to oneself and others, tolerance of differences, and the capacity of each member of the community to grow as a human being and a learner. MindUP's expansive dynamic is built to a large extent on routine practices that are inherent to the MindUP Curriculum. Over the course of the MindUP experience, students learn about the brain and how it functions, in the process gaining insight into their own minds and behaviors as well as those of the people around them.

How Does MindUP Work?

The essential work of MindUP is accomplished through the lessons themselves, which include the repetition of the Core Practice—deep belly breathing and attentive listening. The Core Practice makes mindful attention the foundation for learning and interacting; ideally, it is repeated for a few moments of each school day throughout the year. (See Lesson 3, page 42, for a complete overview of the Core Practice.)

> ## "I love MindUP! It is a way to focus your mind, calm down and reflect on a situation when you need to make a choice."
> ### —Avery, seventh grade

MindUP has the capacity to alter the landscape of your classroom by letting students in on the workings of their own agile minds. Each MindUP lesson begins with background information on the brain, introducing a specific area of concentration with an activity in which students can see concrete examples of how their brain functions. As you and your students become accustomed to learning about the ways in which the brain processes information, your students will become habitually more observant of their own learning process.

MindUP offers teachers and students insights that respond to the natural thoughtfulness of young people and lead to self-regulation of their behavior. MindUP is dedicated to the belief that the child who learns to monitor his or her senses and feelings becomes more aware and better understands how to respond to the world *reflectively* instead of *reflexively*.

Who Needs MindUP?

Everyone. Joyful engagement isn't incidental; it's essential. Yet, young people today are no strangers to stress. From an early age, they experience stress from a range of sources. For some, stress goes hand in hand with the pressure to achieve; for others, it is prompted by economic hardship, poor nutrition, or inadequate health care; for still others, it may be linked to emotional deprivation or limited educational resources. Whatever the particular circumstance, any one of these factors could hamper a student's ability to learn without anxiety. In "communities of turmoil" (Tatum, 2009), children often cope with several problems at once, and suffer from chronic stress—with consequences that can be disastrous for their learning and their lives. MindUP addresses these obstacles to productive learning and living by offering students and teachers simple practices and insights that become tools for self-management and self-possession. At the same time, the MindUP program works to make learning joyful and fun by emphasizing learning modes in which students flourish:

- lively instruction that invites problem solving, discussion, and exploration
- teacher modeling and coaching
- student cross-age mentoring and decision making
- conflict resolution
- inquiry and the arts

Joyful engagement is not incidental; it's essential. MindUP shows you how to put joy into your teaching.

The Research Base

Broadly defined, mindful attention centers on conscious awareness of the present moment: by focusing our attention and controlling our breath, we can learn to reduce stress and optimize the learning capacity of the brain. The use of these practices in MindUP is informed by leading-edge research in the fields of developmental cognitive neuroscience, mindfulness training, social and emotional learning (SEL), and positive psychology. In particular, MindUP pursues objectives roughly parallel to those of the five-point framework of competencies laid out in the work of the Collaborative for Academic, Social, and Emotional Learning (CASEL; www.casel.org), a not-for-profit organization at the forefront in efforts to advance the science- and evidence-based practice of social and emotional learning (SEL). These areas of competency are:

Self-Awareness
Assessing our feelings, interests, values, and strengths; maintaining self-confidence.

Self-Management
Regulating emotions to handle stress, control impulses, and persevere in overcoming obstacles

Social Awareness
Understanding different perspectives and empathizing with others; recognizing and appreciating similarities and differences; using family, school, and community resources effectively

Relationship Skills
Maintaining healthy relationships based on cooperation; resisting inappropriate social pressure; preventing, managing, and resolving interpersonal conflicts; seeking help when needed

Responsible Decision Making
Using a variety of considerations, including ethical, academic, and community-related standards to make choices and decisions

Social and Emotional Learning

It is now well established that social and emotional skills, such as the ability to manage one's emotions and get along with others, play an integral role in academic and life success. Evidence supporting this statement is illustrated in several recent studies. Durlak et al. (2011) conducted a meta-analysis of 213 school-based, universal social and emotional learning (SEL) programs involving 270,034 students from kindergarten through high school and found that, compared to students not exposed to SEL classroom-based programming, students in SEL programs demonstrated significantly improved social and emotional skills, attitudes, behavior, and academic performance that reflected an 11-percentile-point gain in achievement. The importance of SEL in predicting school success has been further demonstrated by Caprara et al. (2000), who found that changes in academic achievement in grade 8 could be better predicted from knowing children's social competence five years earlier than from grade 3 academic competence. As Daniel Goleman, widely recognized as the "founding father" of emotional intelligence (EI), notes, these "remarkable results" make it clear that SEL has "delivered on its promise" (2008).

Adele Diamond, neuroscientist and founder of developmental cognitive neuroscience, found that students who learn SEL techniques such as role-playing consistently score higher on tests requiring use of the brain's executive functions—coordinating and controlling, monitoring and troubleshooting, reasoning and imagining (2007). Similarly, research conducted by social-emotional development expert Kimberly Schonert-Reichl found that "as predicted . . . at posttest teachers in the intervention classrooms described their students as significantly more attentive, emotionally regulated, and socially and emotionally competent than did teachers in the control classrooms" (2010).

As all teachers know, bored children often get into mischief; engaged ones are less likely to act out. Sadly, too often, what students enjoy most is what they get to do the least: discuss, debate, explore the arts, and participate in drama and group research projects. As research demonstrates, "Students experienced a greater level of understanding of concepts and ideas when they talked, explained, and argued about them with their group instead of just passively listening to a lecture or reading a test" (Iidaka et al., 2000). When education is fun, and students are engaged, focused, and inspired to participate, learning flourishes.

SEL programs such as MindUP also significantly impart to students a the sense of hopefulness.

> Hope changes brain chemistry, which influences the decisions we make and the actions we take. Hopefulness must be pervasive and every single student should be able to feel it, see it, and hear it daily (Jensen, 2009; p. 112–113).

Being hopeful mirrors physical activity; both physical activity and hopefulness enhance metabolic states and influence brain-changing gene expression (Jiaxu and Weiyi, 2000). Hope and optimism enable achievement. Hopeful kids are more likely to work diligently and not to give up or drop out—they work harder, persevere longer, and ultimately experience success, which in turn begets more success. It is a simple but profound and life-transforming cycle (Dweck, 2006)—one that is conscientiously cultivated in the MindUP classroom.

The Stressed Brain

The brain's response to stress is linked to the function of the amygdala (uh-MIG-duh-luh), a small, almond-shaped clump of neurons deep in the center of our brain. The amygdala serves as an information filter regulated by our emotional state. When we're calm and peaceful, the filter is wide open and information flows to the prefrontal cortex, where the brain's so-called executive functions take place.

On the other hand, when we are feeling negative and stressed out, these executive functions, or cognitive control, are inhibited. Indeed, information stays in the amygdala; it doesn't flow into the prefrontal cortex for executive processing. Instead, it's processed right on the spot as fight, flight, or freeze. In this way, fear and anxiety effectively shut down higher-order thinking. Your impulse to flee a falling branch, or to defend yourself against physical assault, is an example of your body not bothering to "think about" what to do—you react without thinking.

Eric Jensen, veteran educator and brain expert, in *Teaching With Poverty in Mind: What Being Poor Does to Kids' Brains and What Schools Can Do About It* (2009) has this to say about stress and its effect on the brain:

> The biology of stress is simple in some ways and complex in others. On a basic level, every one of the 30–50 trillion cells in your body is experiencing either healthy or unhealthy growth. Cells cannot grow and deteriorate at the same time. Ideally, the body is in homeostatic balance: a state in which the vital measures of human function—heart rate, blood pressure, blood sugar, and so on—are in their optimal ranges. A stressor is anything that threatens to disrupt homeostasis—for example, criticism, neglect, social exclusion, lack of enrichment, malnutrition, drug use, exposure to toxins, abuse, or trauma. When cells aren't growing, they're in a "hunker down" mode that conserves resources for a threatened future. When billions or trillions of cells are under siege in this manner, you get problems (p. 23).

Neurobiological studies of neglected or abused children have revealed alarming alterations in brain development. The fight-flight-or-freeze stress hormones that our bodies produce in response to physical and emotional adversity "atrophy the areas that control emotional development" (p. 25).

• •

The Happy Brain

To paraphrase Adele Diamond: Happy brains work better (2009).

When we're happy and engaged in activities that we find pleasurable (everything from painting to playing), our brain is flush with dopamine, a neurotransmitter that also helps lubricate our information filter and rev up high-powered thinking in our prefrontal cortex. Dopamine helps get our brains ready for peak performance. Indeed, just the anticipation of pleasurable learning stimulates dopamine flow.

The dopamine pleasure surge is highest when students are fully engaged with their learning and brimming with such positive feelings as optimism, gratitude, hope, and an overall sense of well-being. Classroom activities that give rise to the pleasure surge and prompt the release of dopamine include:

- participating in acts of kindness
- collaborating with peers
- making choices and solving problems
- engaging in physical activities such as sports, dance, and play
- enjoying creative efforts and disciplines such as music, art, drama, reading, and storytelling

Of course, dopamine is also released when people indulge in high-risk activities such as drug or alcohol use, promiscuity, fast driving, and overeating. However, when kids get their pleasure surge from activities that generate positive feelings overall, they are less likely to seek it in high-risk activities that also promote dopamine release (Galvan et al., 2006; Kann et al., 2006).

The Mindful Brain

MindUP is dedicated to helping students deepen their understanding of their own mental processes; the curriculum begins with an introduction to brain physiology. Once students become familiar with the parts of the brain and with how the parts function and interact, they carry that knowledge forward into their MindUP explorations as well as the rest of their classroom experience. The recommended daily Core Practice and the content of each lesson serve as conduits through which young learners can broaden their awareness of the connections between brain and body, between what goes on "inside" and actual experience. The outcome of this is a group of resilient students whose awareness of their impulses, thoughts, feelings, and behavior enhances their confidence, pleasure, and sense of agency in their own learning process.

Consider the benefits that MindUP makes possible! Mindful teaching and learning:

- improve student self-control and self-regulation skills
- strengthen students' resiliency and decision making
- bolster students' enthusiasm for learning
- increase students' academic success
- reduce peer-to-peer conflict
- develop students' positive social skills, such as empathy, compassion, patience, and generosity
- infuse your classroom learning with joy and optimism

MindUP and the School Day

The MindUP program was developed not only to expand students' social and emotional awareness but also to improve their academic performance. The concepts and vocabulary associated with MindUP will expand the scope of students' thinking in all academic disciplines.

MindUP Core Practice can become a staple routine for the opening and closing of each school day as well as at the moments of transition: settling down after recess, waiting for lunch, moving from one subject to the next. As countless MindUP teachers have discovered, any topic benefits from being approached with focused awareness.

The MindUP lessons themselves can be worked smoothly into a daily routine and require minimal preparation on your part; suggested follow-up activities link each lesson to content-area learning. You'll likely find yourself adopting the MindUP techniques and strategies across subject areas. MindUP may well become a way of life for you and your students!

The Day Begins

The best teachers we know are mindful about the beginning of each school day. They make a point of standing by the school door and greeting with an open heart and welcoming smile every student who passes through their classroom door.

An ideal way to unify the class as they begin their day is to gather and share a few moments of "checking in," followed by the Core Practice of deep breathing and mindful awareness. Once you have established this simple routine, you will find that the day feels more coherent and the group less scattered as this practice brings the group together organically while setting an easygoing tone for engagement with the rest of your daily learning.

Transitions

MindUP Core Practice works beautifully during transition times. With your guidance and thoughtful attention, you can accustom your students to respond to a simple reminder at which they automatically turn to the Core Practices to center themselves and prepare to move easily—even eagerly and joyfully—to the next classroom activity. "Our classroom transition times are some of the most important routines of our day….Our days are full, our curriculum is rich, and we have so much to do together! The tighter our transitions, the more time we will have for instruction" (Allyn, 2010).

The Day Ends

Just as you can help students greet a new day with eagerness and mindful purpose, so can you close the day with a similar spirit of purpose and celebration—your students will leave the classroom feeling calm yet energized. Eric Jensen, whose "brain-based" teaching has transformed teaching and learning in countless classrooms, explains, "Asking kids to visualize success on an upcoming skill or knowledge set is no 'new Age' strategy. When done well, mental practice is known not only to make physical changes in the brain but also to improve task performance (Pascual-Leone et al., 2005)" (2010). For example, a spirited and energetic clean-up of the room to some upbeat music can be followed by a regrouping for recapping the day's accomplishments, and a brief shared Core Practice before dismissal. The goal is to end the day on a high note.

MindUP at the Middle Grades

In grades 6–8, students typically travel from class to class, from room to room, and from teacher to teacher. This makes daily Core Practice a challenge, but perhaps also more valuable to the student as he or she juggles the demands of a variety of situations. Ideally, middle-school faculty collaborate to decide which three times to set aside each day for Core Practice. In turn, each middle-school classroom teacher can help students take on more autonomy and more responsibility for their learning by reminding them that during potentially distracting or disruptive transitions, they can take a moment to engage in deep breathing independently to help themselves regain focus. As a content area teacher, in an advisory group, or as study hall monitor, you can incorporate Core Practice into meetings to both calm down and unify the group to focus attention on the subject at hand. Core Practice is an invaluable test preparation tool and an effective brain-readiness habit for approaching any new area of study. MindUP lessons at the middle grades are best taught as the collaborative effort of several instructors and can be coordinated through cross-curricular planning, preferably with the blessing of the school administration.

Literacy expert Pam Allyn has visited and observed hundreds of classrooms around the world. "We have seen many classrooms where there are lots of pieces in place, but one secret, fabulous ingredient is missing. That ingredient is celebration. We see teachers wait to celebrate until the end of the year, until a child does well on a test, until the child actually masters the art of reading. But why wait? Celebration is the ultimate management strategy. . . . It is the core ingredient that infuses the entire life of the classroom with joy, with hope, with faith, and with optimism" (2010, p.107).

Using MindUP in the Classroom

MindUP comprises 15 lessons arranged into four units:

Unit I: Getting Focused (Lessons 1—3)
Introduce brain physiology and the concept of mindful attention; establish daily Core Practice
> **Lessons:** 1. How Our Brains Work, 2. Mindful Awareness,
> 3. Focused Awareness: The Core Practice

Unit II: Sharpening Your Senses (Lessons 4—9)
Experience the relationship between our senses, our moving bodies, and the way we think
> **Lessons:** 4. Mindful Listening, 5. Mindful Seeing, 6. Mindful Smelling,
> 7. Mindful Tasting, 8. Mindful Movement I, 9. Mindful Movement II

Unit III: It's All About Attitude (Lessons 10—12)
Understand the role of our mind-set in how we learn and progress
> **Lessons:** 10. Perspective Taking, 11. Choosing Optimism,
> 12. Appreciating Happy Experiences

Unit IV: Taking Action Mindfully (Lessons 13—15)
Apply mindful behaviors to our interactions with our community and the world
> **Lessons:** 13. Expressing Gratitude, 14. Performing Acts of Kindness,
> 15. Taking Mindful Action in the World

The framework is designed to strengthen students' sense of social and emotional well-being while creating a cohesive, caring classroom environment. Because the concepts build on one another, you'll find it most productive to teach the lessons in sequential order.

Lesson Structure
You'll notice that each lesson follows the same format:

Introduction to the Lesson Topic…identifies and explains the subject of the lesson, frames why it's important, and includes teacher testimony from a MindUP user.

Linking to Brain Research… explains how each lesson relates to the neuroscience. This section provides background for you, which you may want to share with students to help them gain a progressively more sophisticated awareness of how their brains work.

Clarify for the Class… includes guidelines for making brain research concepts accessible to students at various grade levels.

Getting Ready… identifies what the lesson entails as well as learning goals for the lesson. Also listed are materials and resources required for leading the lesson.

MindUP Warm-Up… helps the class prepare for the lesson itself by introducing and discussing subject matter in an easygoing, open-ended way that relates content to students' lives.

Leading the Lesson… offers a step-by-step approach that engages students in the inquiry, helps them explore the topic, and encourages them to reflect upon and discuss their insights and experiences. The lesson layout also establishes concrete links to the learning process and classroom issues at the middle grade level.

Connecting to the Curriculum… offers specific opportunities for students to bend their minds around language arts, math, social studies, science, health, physical education, the arts, and social-emotional learning. These optional across-the-curriculum learning experiences expand the lesson and offer alternative approaches to content.

Special Features

Creating the Optimistic Classroom… offers classroom management strategies for reaching English language learners, special needs students, and general learners in order to maximize the effectiveness of the lesson.

MindUP in the Real World… connects lesson content to a career or undertaking, expands the discussion beyond the classroom setting, and grounds the ideas in a concrete application.

Once a Day… suggests ways for teachers to apply lesson content to everyday situations involving students or colleagues.

Journal Writing… gives students an opportunity to reflect on motivation, actions, and their consequences, so they can learn to mediate and understand their actions. According to Susan Kaiser Greenland, journaling allows students to use what they've learned to create happier, more successful lives for themselves (2010). We recommend that you provide students with a notebook to create a journal that they can personalize with decorations of their choice, using this personal record to document responses within Greenland's general framework of

- What I Noticed
- What It Means
- What I Learned

Literature Link… recommends four books that extend the learning.

Lesson Opener

Each MindUP lesson is focused on one aspect or practice of the curriculum.

The targeted curriculum area is defined and placed in context for the teacher.

Experience of MindUP users attests to the effectiveness of the specific practice or lesson.

Brain research related to lesson exploration is laid out for instructor, along with supporting illustration.

Language and modeling help instructor make the brain research link understandable to students.

Mindful Listening

What Is Mindful Listening?

From the buzz of a cell phone to the wail of a siren, sounds are all around us. Mindful listening helps us choose which sounds to focus our attention on and helps us to be thoughtful in the way we hear and respond to the words of others.

Why Practice Mindful Listening?

Research suggests that students become more focused and responsive to their environment by participating in mindful listening activities, such as Audio Alert in this lesson. In fact, training our brains to concentrate on specific sounds helps heighten our sensory awareness. As students monitor their own auditory experience—noting what they choose to focus on and/or respond to—they build self-awareness and self-management skills. Mindful listening also lays the groundwork for social awareness and effective communication—an important part of the Common Core Standards.

Being able to listen in a focused way to what others say and to home in on details such as tone and inflection gives a listener a clearer notion about the meaning of the words and a better idea for how to respond. This work helps prepare students for following directions, resolving conflicts through discussion, building friendships, and listening critically to news, ads, and other media messages.

What Can You Expect to Observe?

"Students really make an effort tune in to details of the sounds they hear and point out the nuances of sounds that make them distinct. They'll apply mindful listening to observing the way people speak to one another—in particular, identifying the tone of someone's voice and monitoring their own."
—Eighth-grade teacher

Linking to Brain Research

What Is the RAS?

An intricate network of long nerve pathways lies within the core of the brain stem. This reticular formation, also called the reticular activating system (RAS), helps regulate many basic body functions and connects the brain stem to the prefrontal cortex (PFC) and other parts of the brain. The RAS helps keep the brain awake and alert and is the brain's attention-focusing center. Sensory stimuli (visual, auditory, tactile, olfactory, taste) continually arrive via the spinal cord and are sorted and screened by the RAS. The sensory input deemed relevant by the RAS is routed on to its appropriate destination in the conscious brain. What's irrelevant is blocked.

The RAS is critically important because the brain cannot process the millions of bits of sensory information coming in at once! A student sitting in a classroom likely has competing sensory experiences—the voice of her teacher, the vibration of a cell phone, the sight of a friend walking by the classroom, the aroma of food from the cafeteria. It's easy to imagine how these stimuli might cause her to shift her attention from the classroom to what she hopes to eat for lunch. A mindful, focused student is able to reassure herself that lunch period will come after math and to redirect her attention to the task at hand.

Athletes, musicians, scholars, and other "focused" people have "trained" their RAS to choose the most pertinent sensory stimuli. With practice focusing on specific details, students can train their RAS to be more effective. Such practice is especially important for students who have trouble focusing their attention on their work, instructions, or social cues. Sensory awareness activities in this lesson and the others in this unit provide your students with repeated RAS-strengthening practice.

Clarify for the Class

Make a model of the RAS using a kitchen strainer, fine sand, and gravel. Demonstrate how a strainer allows only some things to pass through. Similarly, the RAS holds back unimportant sensory input, but lets relevant information pass on to the PFC.

Discuss: What kinds of sensory input do you think are filtered out by the RAS? (background noise, feeling clothes on body, smell of your own home, etc.) Give examples of situations where you noticed these things. What did you think was happening in your brain at those times?

The RAS serves as an "executive personal secretary" to the PFC, forwarding on only what's immediately relevant.

lesson 4 — mindful listening

Getting Ready

This two-page spread offers an opportunity for preparing and front-loading the main lesson, so that students are most receptive to the language and ideas that follow.

The core lesson ties in with wider self-management and awareness skills. Materials used are basic and usually already available in the classroom or as reproducible pages.

Before each core lesson, a simple preparatory activity helps both teacher and student know what to expect from the lesson and think in advance about how it may be useful in a broader context of learning.

Suggestions for managing classroom, supporting brain-based learning, and helping second language learners address common obstacles to attentiveness and full engagement with learning.

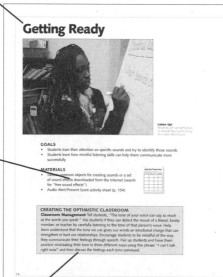

Getting Ready

Listen Up!
Students in a classroom use all the sounds around them to their advantage.

GOALS
- Students train their attention on specific sounds and try to identify those sounds.
- Students learn how mindful listening skills can help them communicate more successfully.

MATERIALS
- various common objects for creating sounds or a set of sound effects downloaded from the Internet (search for "free sound effects")
- Audio Alert/Present Scent activity sheet (p. 154)

CREATING THE OPTIMISTIC CLASSROOM

Classroom Management Tell students, "The tone of your voice can say as much as the words you speak." Ask students if they can detect the mood of a friend, family member, or teacher by carefully listening to the tone of that person's voice. Help them understand that the tone we use gives our words an emotional charge that can strengthen or hurt our relationships. Encourage students to be mindful of the way they communicate their feelings through speech. Pair up students and have them practice modulating their tone in three different ways using the phrase "I can't talk right now" and then discuss the feelings each tone conveyed.

Tuned in to Learning
Training students to focus on one sort of input leaves them more attentive to the primary challenge, such as reading, writing, or solving problems.

MINDUP Warm-Up

Mindful Listening Practice

Build background for this lesson with an auditory-kinesthetic rhythm exercise. Give students a rhythmic clapping and snapping pattern to follow (e.g., clap, snap, snap, clap, snap, clap). Call on students to create their own easy rhythms (three to five beats), then ask them to try increasingly challenging patterns (six to eight beats).

When students are able to come up with unique patterns and repeat the patterns of their peers, organize the class in groups of six to ten and have them play a rhythmic listening game, seated in a circle. Give each group a basic pattern or have the group come up with its own. One at a time, students present a variation on the basic pattern and repeat their new version, cuing the group to repeat their pattern the third time. Suggestions:
- Limit the variations to six or eight beats to avoid too much complexity.
- Model how to make the variation rhythmically interesting by dividing or omitting beats, for example.
- In between turns, encourage the group to return to the original pattern, so it remains fresh in students' minds.

Discuss: What did you have to do in order to keep track of the pattern? How is this kind of listening similar to or different from the kind of listening you do in class? in conversations with friends?

Leading the Lesson

Lessons are supported by findings of educators and researchers on the effectiveness of mindful awareness strategies.

Each lesson routine includes an introduction with scripting to prime students for the exploration and perspective at the core of the teaching.

Core activity of each lesson includes suggested language and procedures to maximize student absorption of the ideas and experience.

At each stage of the lesson, we point out the usefulness of the activity or provide a link to other curriculum areas in which lesson ideas can be implemented.

Lesson focus is extended into its application in the workplace, encouraging students to link learning to the world outside the classroom.

Suggestions for the teacher to incorporate mindful awareness into his or her everyday interactions with colleagues and students.

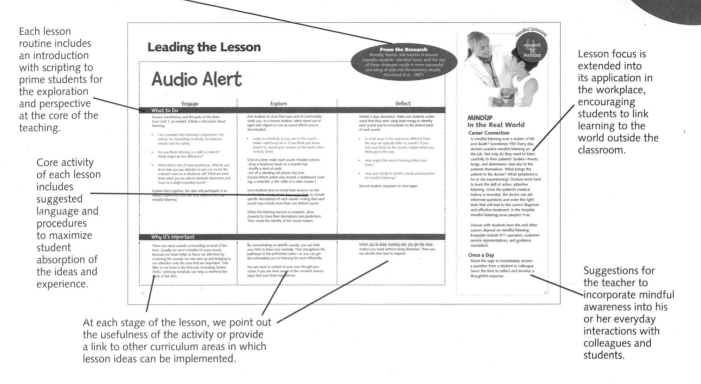

Connecting to the Curriculum

The main lesson is linked to other aspects of students' academic experience: content areas, literature, and writing.

Students are given several prompts for writing and/or drawing in response to the lesson and its target exploration.

Lesson is expanded and extended into three curricular areas and social-emotional learning, connections that can be ongoing as subject-area learning goes on over the course of the school year.

Four literature selections that relate to the lesson focus are recommended for extending the learning.

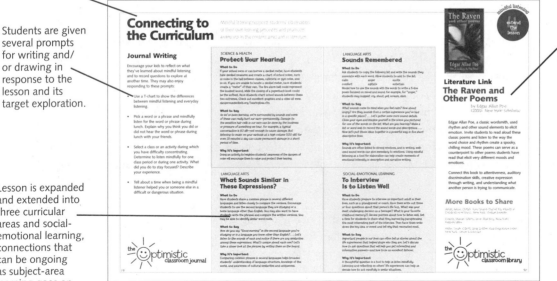

MindUP Implementation

In order to ensure successful implementation of the MindUP program, consider these points:

- MindUP is not a set of strategies to teach in isolation: the curriculum is meant to be an integral part of a complete classroom life. In deciding when to introduce MindUP lessons, consider how to link MindUP to inquiries you are already engaged in from diverse content areas.

- Consider how to set up your classroom with adequate floor space or desk arrangements so that students can see one another. MindUP lessons depend on both whole-group and small-group discussion.

- MindUP lessons draw on students' life experiences and invite students to look closely at their behaviors—for example, their interactions with peers and family. Bear in mind that some students may prefer not to share, for whatever reasons; give students the option to consider their responses privately, or record them in their journals. Additionally, recalling personal experiences, especially for students with challenging lives outside of school, may bring up unsettling emotions. Creating the Optimistic Classroom, featured in each lesson, has classroom management suggestions that address this and other possibly sensitive situations teachers often encounter.

Recommended Implementation Scenarios

MindUP pilot-site teachers have discovered several effective routes to establishing MindUP teaching and practices in their classrooms across the school day and school year. Some of these scenarios are summarized here, followed by an implementation chart to be used for quick reference as you adjust the program to the specific demands of your educational setting, day, and year.

Starting With the Core Practice: Breathe first! From the earliest grades on up, the recommended approach to MindUP is to first establish the habit of deep belly breathing and focused attention—the so-called Core Practice. Well before you teach Lesson 1, you can lay the groundwork for it in your class by introducing the Core Practice in the first days of the school year. Once students have learned the simple techniques of breathing and listening, you will be able to use the Core Practice to unify your classroom community and provide the stability and receptivity needed for days of rich and fruitful learning. The Core Practice is ideally done three times a day (for a few minutes each time), at intervals suggested below but always adjustable to your needs. (See Lesson 3, for a description of the Core Practice.)

- **Pre-K–2:** Use the Core Practice at start of day (during Circle Time), after recess or lunch, and to "regroup" in preparation for dismissal. The Core Practice, which effectively reins in scattered energy, can also serve as an antidote to end-of-day disruptiveness.
- **Grades 3–5:** Use the Core Practice to begin each day, as an introduction to any daily sharing routine or group announcements you may have in place. This simple routine can also be an extremely useful focus and management tool after

recess or lunch, in order to redirect attention to academic subjects—especially before splitting into small groups for collaborative projects.

Because the Core Practice is aimed in part at making the mind more receptive to learning for understanding, it is an ideal tool before embarking on a new area of study or in preparation for tests that are likely to demand that students "keep their cool" while being asked to summon up stored information.

The Core Practice can be built into your routine summing-up of the day, especially as a means for reunifying the class prior to dismissal. The Core Practice by its nature precludes conflict; it is especially effective as a self-regulating skill for upper-elementary students, who are about to experience dramatic physical and emotional changes they may not be well prepared to deal with.

- **Grades 6–8:** By middle school, students are capable of engaging in the Core Practice on their own. As a homeroom, advisory, or content-area instructor, you may wish to build the Core Practice into your class meeting to establish important stability in preparation for the "gear shifting" required as students move among multiple subjects, rooms, and teachers.

  Because the Core Practice prepares the ground for learning, make a point to remind students that they can use it for their own self-regulation and focus when they feel it necessary. This sense of agency is critical for students at this age, as they learn to take responsibility for their own learning and social interactions. In addition, when implementing MindUP at the middle grades, it is extremely helpful to coordinate with other teachers a grade-wide or school-wide plan for incorporating MindUP Core Practice into classroom routines in various contexts across the curriculum and throughout the year.

- **Alternative and Pullout Settings:** The Core Practice is a natural to begin and end sessions in after-school, English-language learning, or special needs settings. It brings calm, unity, and focus to individuals and groups, and sets the stage for introducing almost any area of study or collaborative activity.

MindUP Lessons

The 15 MindUP lessons can be presented at regular intervals and in diverse forms throughout the typical 32-week school year.

In the first few weeks of the year, as explained earlier, "Breathe first!" can be your motto. This is the time for students to become acquainted with the Core Practice and habituated to the daily experience of mindful listening and focused attention to their own breathing and thought processes. By the end of about three weeks, classroom routines and schedules are in place and students have adjusted to the new academic profile. At this point you can begin to launch the MindUP curriculum in earnest, working through the program in sequence from Unit I.

Implementation Scenarios: The following recommendations are based on the experience of MindUP pilot teachers at all grade levels. "Chunking" the lessons is entirely adaptable to your classroom needs; below is an approximation of how to approach incorporating MindUP into the generally busy days all teachers face.

Review thoroughly the information in Linking to Brain Research on the second page of the lesson. Plan at least one 15-minute chunk of time to familiarize students with this material, which always deals with some aspect of how the brain works; a second 15-minute session may be advisable in order to solidify that learning.

Getting Ready, on pages 3 and 4 of the lesson, can also be treated as a learning chunk to be repeated or extended as necessary in advance of the core lesson, outlined on the following two pages. The MindUP warm-up is an opportunity to refer back to the Brain Research segment, and to reinforce students' Core Practice competencies as they prepare for the lesson.

Leading the Lesson may take place over a few days, depending on how much time you are able to devote to it. You may wish to treat Engage and Explore as one chunk, then move on to Reflect and MindUP in the Real World in a separate meeting. If you have the time to rewind a bit and incorporate previous discoveries, students will gain from the recap and reinforcement.

The final two pages of the lesson are the most open-ended in terms of time chunking. The adaptability of lesson content to other curriculum areas and the extension of the lesson into reading and writing activities are important assets of MindUP. These extensions can be carried out in several chunks, feasibly encompassing parts of several days or weeks, depending on the organization of your academic curriculum.

> **Unit I** In most classrooms, teachers have found that the Unit I lessons are best introduced in concentrated doses over the course of approximately two weeks each, spending time to become familiar with the brain basics. The self-regulatory routine of the Core Practice will serve as a backdrop for students' discoveries about what is going on inside as they learn and interact. Because the material here is concrete "science information," it may be best to set aside 30 minutes at a time, in order to be able to discuss and review as needed.

> **Units II and III** These lessons, numbered 4 through 12, can be covered in 15-minute chunks, extending over approximately two weeks. You may wish to occasionally use a 30- to 45-minute period to go into depth on lesson segments. However, since a fundamental purpose of MindUP is to apply mindful awareness in other areas of the curriculum and parts of the school day, there is a benefit to working MindUP knowledge into other discussions and practices. The final two pages of each lesson offer specific applications of the lesson to other parts of the students' academic experience.

> **Unit IV** The final three lessons are geared toward reaching beyond the immediate context of a lesson, applying MindUP insights to behaviors and actions in the larger community or the world. For these lessons, the time frame can be more open-ended, with classroom discussions serving as an anchor for independent work and reflection on how students' skills at self-regulation, self-discipline, and self-examination have affected their confidence and competence.

At each grade level, there are key factors to consider when implementing MindUP.

- **Pre-K–2:** At the earliest grades, a predominant focus of the program will be on the development of self-regulation skills. Children are usually eager to become skilled practitioners of the Core Practice at these early grades. Once the Core Practice has been established, children become more receptive to and engaged in learning in all areas, and more successful at integrating the academic and social considerations of school life. Keeping MindUP an adventurous exploration rooted in self-awareness is key to helping children enjoy and apply the exciting knowledge they will acquire.

- **Grades 3–5:** Students' broadening self-awareness during this period dovetails well with MindUP's introduction of brain science to broaden the base of students' core knowledge. Learning about their own thinking and gaining some control over their thought processes are useful not only for taking in new information but also for responding, as on standardized testing, to somewhat stressful demands that they "show what they know."

- **Grades 6–8:** At middle school, students will increasingly be able to use MindUP as a tool to prepare themselves to learn. As they acquire agency over their own learning and determine with greater independence how to direct their energies, use their time, organize their lives, and interact with their peers, students in grades 6–8 can look to MindUP for both knowledge and practical skills over the course of a school day and school year.

Alternative Settings: MindUP can be implemented in after-school programs as well as in pullout programs for special needs students or English language learners. The focus in these settings can be on the establishment of the Core Practice; by doing this, you can establish a setting that is receptive to learning—for each student as well as for the group as a whole. Core Practice can become the beginning and end practice each time you meet; you can reinforce the concepts and principles of MindUP by reminding students of the self-regulation tools at their disposal, as well as the mindful attention they can make habitual in every learning situation.

For all students, paying attention to their own thinking process and behaviors consistently enhances receptivity to learning in other academic and social-emotional areas.

Implementation Charts

Sample MindUP Lesson Chunking for Grades Pre-K–2 and 3–5

Time	Chunk/Content	Lesson pg
10–15 min	Linking to Brain Research & Clarify for the Class	2
10–15 min	Getting Ready, MindUP Warm-Up & Discuss	3–4
10–15 min	Leading the Lesson: Engage & Explore	5
10–15 min	Leading the Lesson: Reflect & MindUP in the Real World	6
(variable)	Extend: Journal Writing*	7
10–15 min	Extend: Connecting to Curriculum*	7–8
10–15 min	Extend: Connecting to Curriculum*	7–8
(variable)	Extend: Literature Link (Independent Reading)*	8

* It is highly recommended that you take advantage of extension links, in order to apply MindUP principles to support and facilitate all kinds of learning.

Sample MindUP Lesson Chunking for Grades 6–8

Time	Chunk/Content	Lesson pg
10–15 min	Linking to Brain Research & Clarify for the Class	2
10–15 min	Getting Ready, MindUP Warm-Up & Discuss	3–4
10–15 min	Leading the Lesson: Engage & Explore	5
10–15 min	Leading the Lesson: Reflect & MindUP in the Real World	6
(variable)	Extend: Journal Writing*	7
10–15 min	Extend: Connecting to Curriculum*	7–8
10–15 min	Extend: Connecting to Curriculum*	7–8
(variable)	Extend: Literature Link (Independent Reading)*	8

* It is highly recommended that you take advantage of extension links, in order to apply MindUP principles to support and facilitate all kinds of learning. (Curriculum links may be handled by content area instructors.)

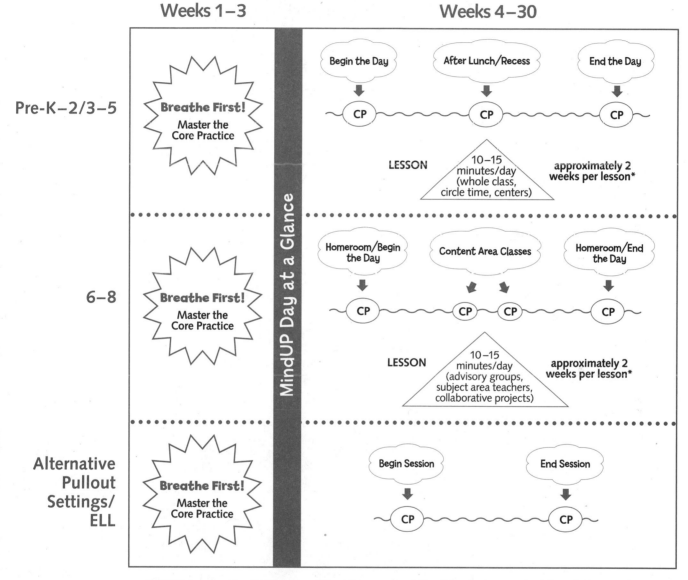

Weeks 1–3

Weeks 4–30

Pre-K–2/3–5

6–8

Alternative Pullout Settings/ ELL

MindUP Day at a Glance

Breathe First!
Master the Core Practice

Begin the Day   After Lunch/Recess   End the Day

CP   CP   CP

LESSON   10–15 minutes/day (whole class, circle time, centers)   approximately 2 weeks per lesson*

Breathe First!
Master the Core Practice

Homeroom/Begin the Day   Content Area Classes   Homeroom/End the Day

CP   CP   CP   CP

LESSON   10–15 minutes/day (advisory groups, subject area teachers, collaborative projects)   approximately 2 weeks per lesson*

Breathe First!
Master the Core Practice

Begin Session   End Session

CP   CP

* NOTE: Lessons 14 and 15 require student time spent outside of the classroom; schedule and duration of these lessons should be adjusted accordingly.

CP=Core Practice

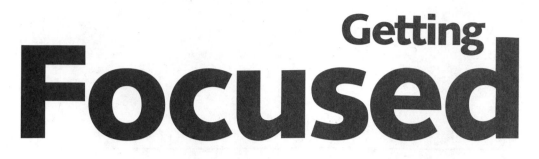

Getting
Focused

By learning how their brains respond to stress and by practicing strategies for quieting their minds, students become better at self-regulating, increase their capacity for absorbing information, and improve their relationship skills.

Children learn about the three parts of their brains that help them think and respond to stress.

Children compare two types of behavior—mindful (reflective and purposeful) and unmindful (reflexive and unaware)—and identify the parts of the brain responsible for controlling each type.

This lesson introduces daily strategies for calming down and paying attention. Children begin to learn ways to help their brains work more mindfully.

Do you ever wonder why high-pressure situations make us "lose our cool"? An accelerated heartbeat and butterflies in the stomach seem to happen no matter how well prepared we are.

The human brain is wired to respond to stress as if something were immediately threatening, often placing us at the mercy of our physical and emotional responses. Yet, we can actually train our brains to respond reflectively. This realization is empowering for students, who deal with many stresses in and out of the classroom—from bullying to homework.

The focus of this unit is on the interplay of three key parts of the brain—the amygdala (reactive center), the prefrontal cortex (reflective center), and the hippocampus (memory and information storage center). Children will learn practical strategies, including listening and breathing exercises, to prime their brains for learning and behaving mindfully.

How Our Brains Work

What's So Important About the Brain?

Our brain can serve as a map for showing us how we learn and why we behave the way we do. Neuroscience provides a wealth of information that can help us and our students become better thinkers and healthier people.

Why Introduce Students to Brain Research?

Students are fascinated by facts about their brains. Sharing scientific information about how the brain processes information and is wired to react under stress is a great way to introduce a challenge to your students: How can we learn to react differently, helping our brain make wise choices about our words and actions?

As students become more familiar with three key parts of the brain involved in thinking and learning, they'll begin to understand how their feelings arise—and that they have the ability to change what they do in response. This understanding lays the groundwork for them to monitor and regulate their behavior by calming themselves in the face of anxiety, focusing their attention, and taking control of their learning.

What Can You Expect to Observe?

"Students are amazed and relieved that their brains are not some kind of black box. Learning about the parts and functions of the brain gives students insight and control over what is going on in there. This is a pretty big idea for students who often feel fairly ravaged by emotion."

—Seventh-grade teacher

Linking to Brain Research

Meet Some Key Players in the Brain

The limbic system controls emotions and motivations from deep inside the brain. A key player of the limbic system is the amygdala. The amygdala is a pair of almond-shaped structures that reacts to fear, danger, and threat. The amygdala regulates our emotional state by acting as the brain's "security guard," protecting us from threats. When a student is in a positive emotional state, the amygdala sends incoming information on to the conscious, thinking, reasoning brain. When a student is in a negative emotional state (stressed or fearful, for example) the amygdala prevents the input from passing along, effectively blocking higher-level thinking and reasoned judgment. The incoming stimuli and signals are left for the amygdala itself to process as an automatic reflexive response of "fight, flight, or freeze."

The hippocampus is another limbic system structure. These twin crescent-shaped bodies reside in the central brain area, one behind each ear, in the temporal lobes. The hippocampus assists in managing our response to fear and threats, and is a storage vault of memory and learning.

Information from the limbic system is fed to the prefrontal cortex—the learning, reasoning, and thinking center of the brain. This highly evolved area of the brain controls our decision making, focuses our attention, and allows us to learn to read, write, compute, analyze, predict, comprehend, and interpret.

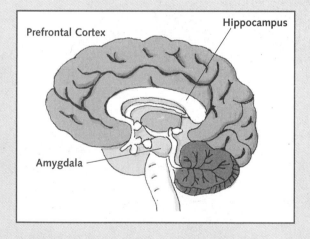

Learning about these key players helps students understand how their brains respond to stress and prepares them for creating a calm mind-set for thoughtful decision making, led by the prefrontal cortex.

Clarify for the Class

Make a model to show how the brain processes information under stress. Fill a clear plastic bottle with water, an inch of sand, some glitter, and metallic mini-confetti. To demonstrate the way the amygdala on alert scatters information, shake the bottle and mix up the solution. The settling solution represents the calming mind. Explain to students that, eventually, the bits of information that at first seem so chaotic flow in a clear direction, some of them to the PFC for thoughtful decision making.

Discuss: Name a time when you felt stressed out and your mind was functioning more or less like the shaken bottle. What helped you think clearly and focus?

Getting Ready

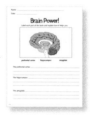

Big Brain
This lesson's introduction can serve as a jumping off point for students to do further research about the brain for science or health class.

GOALS
- Students will identify three parts of the brain: the amygdala, the hippocampus, and the prefrontal cortex (PFC) on a diagram of the brain.
- Students will arrive at a simple definition of each of these three parts.

MATERIALS
- chart paper
- MindUP poster "Getting to Know and Love Your Brain"
- Brain Power! activity sheet (p. 152)

CREATING THE OPTIMISTIC CLASSROOM
Classroom Management As students observe how stress interferes with thinking, create classroom habits that foster calm reflection.
- Remind students not to talk over you or each other and to give everyone a chance to be heard.
- Pause for a moment before calling on students to answer questions.
- Give students the option of answering with, "I need to think about that some more," and then scheduling a time to return to the discussion.
- Encourage students to take a moment to write notes before group discussions.
- Allow students to formulate follow-up questions after they have had time to digest learning.

Brain Habits
Students enjoy a "brain mini-challenge:" miming familiar tasks, such as brushing their teeth, with their nondominant hand.

MINDUP Warm-Up

Mind Skills Discussion

Ask students to think about how people acquire different skills. Get the discussion started by offering an example or two—a basketball player practicing free throws, a pianist warming up with scales, and so on.

Give students a few moments to think. Then ask students to put both hands in the air when they're ready with an example. Toss a crumpled piece of paper, or other soft object, toward one pair of raised hands. The student who catches the object gives his or her example. Have that student make the next toss. Continue until all volunteers have shared. Be sure to model attentive listening during this exercise.

Discuss the role of mind skills in various activities. In sports, you can't let yourself get psyched out during the game. If you're performing, you can't afford to freeze up with stage fright. Discuss further examples offered by students.

Explain that MindUP lessons will help students develop mind skills—ways to rev up their minds for new ideas and to calm them down and focus in order to concentrate! Lead students to discover that mind skills are especially important in school.

Discuss: What kind of skill drills could you invent that would help you be creative or help you concentrate?

Leading the Lesson

Team Brain

Engage	Explore

What to Do

Using handouts of the Brain Power! activity sheet and the "Getting to Know and Love Your Brain" poster for reference, introduce the three key parts of the brain: the prefrontal cortex, the amygdala, and the hippocampus.

- Parts of the brain operate like a team, each part with a position and job to do.

Have students make two fists and join them at the knuckles with the thumbs facing them. Explain that this is a decent model of the approximate size and configuration of their brain, which is divided into two hemispheres. The thumbs represent the prefrontal cortex (thinking). The tips of the index finger are the amygdalae (emotions), and the tips of the middle fingers are the hippocampus (memories).

Present the analogy of a football team. Assign a position on the team to each of the three parts of the brain you've discussed. Point out the link between position and function for each "player."

- Imagine the prefrontal cortex as the quarterback. It helps you pay attention and make good choices.

- Imagine the amygdala as a blocker. It's alert to danger and keeps you safe. It also expresses emotions, such as anger and fear. Sometimes the blocker can move too quickly or with too much roughness and cause a penalty.

- Imagine the hippocampus as the coach. It remembers the old games and has the playbook. It retrieves important information that has been stored for later use.

Think of a situation that is typically challenging for students, such as taking a test. Invite students to stage a short play that shows how these brain parts might work together in such a situation.

Why It's Important

Using analogies and models to establish the locations of the brain parts captures students' interest, reinforces concepts in several different ways, and helps them build a foundation for future lessons.

It's important to understand that while the amygdala can help keep us safe, sometimes it signals danger when there is none. When that happens, our ability to think clearly is hampered because the passage of information to the PFC is blocked.

From the Research
Students are more likely to remember and really understand what they learn if they find it compelling or have some part in figuring it out or discovering some part of it for themselves.
(Willis, 2008)

Reflect

To review, have students pair up and retell in their own words the function of each brain part. Then have them fill in the name of each part on the activity sheet and explain its function. Encourage students to add notes and words that help them remember what each part does.

Share another challenging scenario to ensure that students can identify the brain parts and their functions.

- Imagine you are walking to school and you see ahead of you, blocking the sidewalk, a large group of bigger kids you don't know. How does your body immediately react? What are you thinking? What experience can you draw on?

- What does your brain's quarterback (the prefrontal cortex) do? What does your brain's blocker (the amygdala) do? What does your brain's coach (the hippocampus) do?

Explain that future MindUP lessons will help students use their brain team effectively. They will be able to assess situations and calm their amygdala if there's no real danger, strengthen their ability to focus and get information to the PFC, and store important ideas in their hippocampus.

Using real-life scenarios to show the different parts of the brain in action helps students organize and apply information about the brain. This review lays the groundwork for the next lesson, which connects mindful and unmindful behaviors to the roles of the amygdala and PFC.

MINDUP
In the Real World

Career Connection

If you're fascinated by the brain and how it works, you might consider a career as a neuroscientist. A neuroscientist is anyone who studies the brain and central nervous system. Within the wide-ranging field of neuroscience, there are many specialized jobs; for example, a *neuroanatomist* studies the structure of the nervous system, while a *neurochemist* investigates how neurotransmitters work. If operating on the brain sounds exciting, consider the work of a *neurosurgeon*, or, if you're concerned about diseases that affect the brain, become a *neuropathologist*. A *neuropsychologist* explores brain-behavior relationships.

Discuss: If you could choose one job with the prefix *neuro-* or *brain* in the job title, what would it be and why?

Once a Day

Pick a specific time to stop and self-assess: Do your responses reveal the involvement of your amygdala (reaction) or your PFC (reflection)? If your amygdala is being activated, what is triggering its response? What would you like to change about your style reaction?

Connecting to the Curriculum

Learning about the brain supports students' connection to their own learning process and to the content areas and literature.

Journal Writing

Encourage your students to reflect on what they've learned about how their brains think and learn and to record questions to explore at another time. They may also enjoy responding to these prompts:

- Draw a cartoon of the usual mode of action of your own amygdala. Below your picture, describe how your amygdala most often reacts to danger. Is your amydgala more like a runner, a statue, or a fighter?

- Try a before-and-after experiment. Describe how your PFC is working right now. Then use your hippocampus to focus on an especially happy memory. Do you notice any effect on your PFC's functioning? Do you feel calmer? Is your thinking clearer?

- Imagine that your amygdala is overre-acting. There really is no danger. Write a conversation among your PFC, amygdala, and hippocampus. What would they say to each other?

- Write about a time when you helped someone calm down. Think about the kinds of things you did and said. What worked best? What didn't work at all?

the Optimistic classroom™ journal

HEALTH
Safety First!

What to Do
Challenge students to become "brain safety experts" by having them brainstorm things that could hurt their brains and research ways to keep their brains safe. Invite them to use classroom resources, the Web, or library books. Have students take notes and group their information into categories, such as brain safety and sports or brain safety and drugs.

What to Say
You have more reasons than ever to care about your brain's safety, now that you've learned about it's important functions— it makes decisions, keeps you out of danger, and stores your memories. Can you think of an advertisement that will get people's attention and help them take brain safety seriously? You can work with a partner or a small group and we can share them when you're done.

Why It's Important
Inviting students to learn about brain safety can make them more aware of risky behaviors and what the possible consequences might be. By having students engage in a persuasive exercise, you will help give them the language they need to walk away from destructive behaviors suggested by peers.

LANGUAGE ARTS
Vocabulary Synapses

What to Do
This activity will help students mirror how information links up inside the brain. Have students start with two words whose meanings have no connection to each other whatsoever, such as *penguin* and *radio*. Have students brainstorm words associated with each "trunk" word to try to get the two to eventually connect.

What to Say
Write each starter word on a separate piece of paper. Draw "branches" coming off your trunk word; on each branch write a word you associate with the trunk word. See if you can eventually interconnect the branches between trunk words. For a challenge, write on the branch what the relationships are: synonyms, antonyms, same category of thing, and so on.

Why It's Important
Demonstrating how information is organized by the hippocampus gives students a powerful mental model about information storing, which will be useful in upcoming lessons.

SCIENCE
Gray Matter Glossary

What to Do
Have students make a word list of brain words. They can start with the words in this lesson and gather others from classroom sources, the Web, or the library books. *Neurons, synapses,* and *hemispheres* are some suggestions to get them started. You may wish to use a shoe box as a gathering point and have students create their glossary on index cards. That way their work can be combined into a class resource.

What to Say
See how many brain terms you can collect and define. Feel free to use images that help you communicate the meaning. Also feel free to use the football team analogy. For example, neurotransmitters are the chemical messages that travel from one brain cell to another. They are like a ball that is passed.

Why It's Important
Learning more brain vocabulary will support students' learning in the life sciences. At the same time, they will acquire language to talk about what is going on in their own brains and the ways in which they can take some control of those processes.

SOCIAL-EMOTIONAL LEARNING
Doom or Dud

What to Do
Help students recognize when their amygdala is overreacting, a "worst-case scenario" test. Hand each student two strips of paper. Have students write down two situations that might prompt their amygdala to signal danger—one situation in which the danger is real and one in which it is not. Instruct students to fold up their strips and put them in a paper bag.

What to Say
Pick a strip at random from the bag and answer each of the following questions for the scenario it describes: What is the worst thing that could happen? What is the best thing that could happen? What is most likely to happen?. . .Listen to your classmates' assessments of the situations. Let's link our responses to the roles of the amygdala, PFC, and hippocampus.

Why It's Important
Recognizing real danger quickly is critical to students' safety. However, being able to put aside anxieties and worries, which negatively impact health and learning, is also an important skill.

Literature Link
The Great Brain Book

by H.P. Newquist
(2004). New York: Scholastic.

This engaging book offers insights into how our knowledge of brain function has changed over the years. Colorful, detailed diagrams and colorful artwork enhance the discussion.

Throughout, kid-friendly details are provided such as how tightrope walkers rewire their fear centers to perform or why we experience "brain freeze" after eating something cold.

More Books to Share

Bagert, Brod. (2006). *Hormone Jungle: Coming of Age in Middle School.* New York: Maupin House.

Holbrook, Sara. (2003). *By Definition: Poems of Feelings.* Honesdale, PA: Boyds Mills Press.

Howe, James. (2006). *13: Thirteen Stories That Capture the Agony and Ecstasy of Being Thirteen.* New York: Atheneum Books.

the **Optimistic** classroom™ library

Mindful
Awareness

What Is Mindful Awareness?

Attending to the here and now—other people, the environment, a concern or challenge—in a considerate, nonjudgmental way is called mindful awareness. It's a skill that can be developed by paying close attention to our present situation and our role in it. By reflecting on our thoughts and actions, we can decide how to make better choices when appropriate.

Why Introduce Students to Mindful Awareness?

Learning to be mindfully in tune with what's happening in the moment prepares students to make sound decisions rather than be ruled by their emotions. In Lesson 1, students learned that their brains can produce a well-thought-out reaction by way of the reflective prefrontal cortex or trigger a thoughtless one through the reflexive amygdala. In this lesson, students further explore those contrasting styles of response, using the terms *mindful* and *unmindful* to sort out important thoughts and actions in their own lives. They also discuss the benefits of mindful awareness and learn a focusing strategy for being more mindful.

This lesson provides the language of self-awareness, self-control, and compassionate action that undergirds the rest of MindUP.

What Can You Expect to Observe?

"Using the words 'mindful' and 'unmindful' in the classroom has helped us discuss classroom behavior in a way that reduces defensiveness.... It also helps when students understand that we all behave in mindful and unmindful ways throughout the day."

—Eighth-grade teacher

Linking to Brain Research

The Amygdala and Mindful Awareness

The **amygdala** determines emotional responses by classifying incoming sights, sounds, smells, and movements as either potentially threatening or pleasurable. Input deemed pleasurable goes on to the prefrontal cortex where it is analyzed *before* it is responded to. Input perceived as threatening is blocked by the amygdala and instead prompts an immediate reflexive reaction—fight, flight, or freeze.

The amygdala does not make a distinction between perceived threats and actual dangers. It can trigger "false alarm" reactive behavior that is unwarranted and potentially problematic. For instance, we sometimes freeze in stressful situations, such as taking a test. This is an example of unmindful behavior. A reaction happens before the mind thinks about it. Conversely, when we consciously process sensory input, we create a time buffer between the input and the response. This gives the prefrontal cortex time to analyze, interpret, and prioritize information, allowing us to choose the best course of action. We call this mindful behavior. A response happens *after* our mind has thought about it.

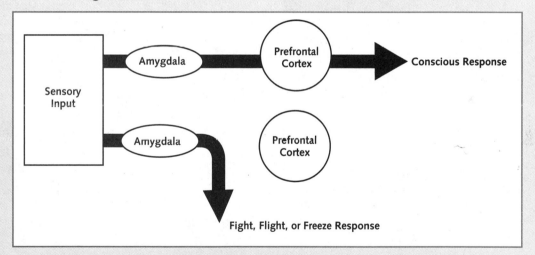

Unmindful thoughts and actions occur when the gate-keeper amygdala blocks the flow of sensory input to the prefrontal cortex and unconsciously reacts.

Clarify for the Class

Explain that mindful thinking results when the prefrontal cortex is allowed to process sensory information that arrives at the amygdala. An example is "counting to ten" when you're frustrated or angry. Counting gives the amygdala time to allow the input to move on to the prefrontal cortex and be analyzed more accurately.

Discuss: Have any of you ever been asked to count to ten when angry? Did it help? Why? What do you think was happening in the amygdala and the prefrontal cortex at "1" and later at "10"?

Getting Ready

What's the Evidence?
Having students evaluate a persuasive argument for evidence is a way to help them build mindful evaluation skills.

GOALS

- Students define and describe the difference between mindful and unmindful thoughts and actions.
- Students apply the concept of mindful awareness to their own lives.

MATERIALS

- chart paper
- index cards or scratch paper
- Mindful or Unmindful? activity sheet (p. 153)

CREATING THE OPTIMISTIC CLASSROOM

Classroom Management At the end of the lesson, record on chart paper students' reminders about mindful behavior. Post these reminders on chart paper or a bulletin board so that the class can refer to them during discussions and conflict resolutions. Statements might include:

- I can get into the habit of noticing what my mind is doing.
- If my mind is drifting, I can try to refocus it.
- If my amygdala is acting up over something that isn't serious, I can try to quiet it down.
- If I am rushing to make judgments, I can go back to just noticing and taking in more information.

Strike!
Any game of skill that requires
concentration is a great way to
demonstrate how to focus
attention.

MINDUP Warm-Up

Poetry Aloud Focus Practice

Use this auditory focusing exercise to demonstrate how to maintain mindful focus.

Ask students to listen to the following poem and try and hold the details of it in their
mind during 30 seconds of silence. Then ask students to list or draw all the details
they can remember. Give students a few moments to share their results.

Fog (from *Chicago Poems* by Carl Sandberg)

> The fog comes
> on little cat feet.
> It sits looking
> over harbor and city
> on silent haunches
> and then moves on.

Discuss: When you try to keep your mind focused, it often tries to wander. How can
you keep your mind focused on the details that you choose? How can having this
kind of control help you?

Leading the Lesson

Mindful, Yes or No?

Engage

What to Do

Reflect on the warm-up exercise. Connect it to what students have learned about the brain.

- How hard or easy was it to keep your mind focused for 30 seconds? You might have struggled a little to keep your PFC focused on the poem and keep your amygdala calm. If you were successful, the details could make it to the hippocampus, which saves the memory.

Explain that focusing our attention on what's happening here and now is part of being mindful, or paying close attention. The second part of being mindful is suspending judgment—keeping an open mind and waiting to form an opinion until you have considered a situation more carefully.

- Making quick judgments about things and people is a very popular thing to do in our society: In or out? Hot or not? Who's got talent? Part of being mindful is to suspend judgment in order to take in more information. A good judge needs to hear and see all the important evidence. Not everything is the way it seems at first. Can you think of an example?

Why It's Important

Making judgments is an important part of learning to think critically. Students should learn to make sound judgments based on evidence. Mindful awareness can be described as "noticing without rushing to judgment." Mindful awareness allows students to gather important evidence in order to make better judgments.

Explore

What to Do

Help students differentiate between mindful behavior and its opposite, unmindful behavior. Share an example to contrast the two.

- A mindful approach to making friends would be getting to know the positions of both candidates for class president. An unmindful approach would be deciding to vote for someone because your friends are voting for that person.

- How would you describe the difference between these two approaches?

Read each example from the Mindful or Unmindful? activity sheet and have students vote on whether the behavior described seems mindful or unmindful. If the behavior is unmindful, have them brainstorm with a partner about how it could be made mindful.

- Consider which of these examples show thinking and acting in a way that is attentive and not judgmental.

Why It's Important

Having students evaluate familiar actions such as the ones described on the activity sheet helps them begin to make connections between mindful awareness and their own habits and choices.

Be careful not to let this exercise be used to make students feel judged. Emphasize that everyone goes through the day with a mixture of mindful and unmindful behaviors.

Reflect

Invite students to share a mindful experience that they have had. It could be something serious like listening to a friend who was upset, or just walking carefully on a rocky beach. Discuss what it felt like.

Remind students that all of us are occasionally unmindful then invite volunteers to share an experience when someone else was acting unmindfully—for example, being interrupted by someone or having someone let a door close in your face. Discuss what that felt like.

- Being mindful takes effort. We're all going to practice being more mindful together and no one is going to be perfect.

- When we notice unmindful behavior in ourselves, we can say, "Please excuse me, I wasn't using my PFC." When we notice it in others, we can gently and politely say, "Calling all PFCs!"

Conclude this lesson by creating a class toolbox to post to help students become mindful when they are struggling with it. (See Creating the Optimistic Classroom box, page 36.)

Encouraging students to recall examples of mindful and unmindful behavior helps model when extra attention might be needed. Being unmindful is not the same as making a negative choice. Being unmindful probably means our amygdala is in charge or our PFC is wandering. Being more mindful can make us, and the people around us, safer, healthier, and happier.

MINDUP In the Real World

Career Connection

At the first wail of an ambulance siren, an EMT, often the first to arrive at the scene of an accident, is trained to remain calm and focus on what has happened and what immediate action is required. EMTs are typically dispatched to an emergency scene by a 911 operator and often work with police or fire departments. All EMTs must know how to assess an emergency, control bleeding, apply splints, assist with childbirth, administer oxygen, and perform CPR and other basic life-support skills. Mindfulness that enables quick, decisive thinking is the EMT's most essential skill.

Discuss: Think of five other high-pressure jobs, such as air-traffic controlling, where split-second decisions must be made mindfully.

Once a Day

Share with students an observation about a mindful decision you or a student made in a demanding situation. Reflect on how your PFC may have guided the wise choice.

Connecting to the Curriculum

Learning about mindful behavior supports students' connection to their own learning process and to the content areas and literature.

Journal Writing

Encourage your students to reflect on what they've learned about being mindful and to record questions to explore at another time. They may also enjoy responding to these prompts:

- Write an acrostic for MINDFUL, using each letter in the word to make a statement about being mindful with a word that has the same initial letter. You might use a repeating pattern, such as: *M* is for staying in the moment, *I* is for....

- Being unmindful can be bad for your health. Draw a picture of someone being unmindful in a risky way. Write a caption that describes what the person is doing and why it is dangerous.

- Write a letter to someone, apologizing for a time when you were unmindful. Explain how you plan to be more mindful in the future.

- Imagine your mindful attention taking the form of a bull's-eye. Whatever is in the center is what you are most mindful of. Use words and images in the rings to represent your attention on most days.

the Optimistic classroom™ journal

SOCIAL STUDIES
Mindful Travels

What to Do
Explain to students that being mindful can get more complicated when you interact with people from different parts of the world. For example, in some cultures it would be very rude to show the bottom of your shoes. If you were traveling to Middle East, you would want to be mindful of that. Have students pick a country to research and make a list of things to be mindful of there.

What to Say
Now you're learning about being mindful at home and at school. But when you travel, especially to a foreign country, there are many things to be mindful of. The cars may use the opposite side of the street. The history of the place may include events that make people uncomfortable, or they may have opinions about where YOU come from! How can you be mindful in new cultures? Pick an unfamiliar place and find out about its customs and history in order to mindfully prepare for an imaginary trip!

Why It's Important
Being mindful is a great interpersonal skill. It can be used in familiar environments and in new ones too. Part of travel is to discover new things. Being observant and suspending judgment can be important aspects of that.

LANGUAGE ARTS
Mindful Play

What to Do
Students can practice their creative writing skills while they practice their mindful skills. Present a scenario, such as one friend texting while the other is talking. Then have students write a short play about that. Have the friends interact. Encourage students to explore what might be said. What could they discover about being mindful?

What to Say
Have you sat waiting while a friend talked on the phone or was texting someone? Have you ever done that to a friend? Think about how each person might feel. As you write your play, try to think of a twist. Try to factor in something about the situation that is not exactly as it seems!

Why It's Important
Composing scripts for situations in which mindful behavior is an issue can give students an opportunity to strategize different approaches. They can test out alternatives and learn what might work best for them.

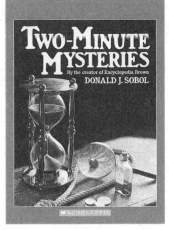

MATH
Measuring is Mindful

What to Do
Explain to students that math is a great way to describe things without using language "loaded" with snap judgments. Math can describe things by their geometric shape or by measurements. Have students choose an object in the classroom to describe using only mathematical terms.

What to Say
Mindful awareness is the ability to notice and suspend judgment while you collect information. See if your classmates can identify the object you describe using the language of math. You can use geometric shapes, ratios, perimeters, areas, and any other measures that apply. We will post and number all mindful measurements. We will see how many people can recognize objects this way.

Why It's Important
This activity is a good opportunity for students to look at things in a new way. Being mindful is a way of paying attention that is great practice for objective subjects, such as math and science, that require information and patience before drawing conclusions.

SOCIAL-EMOTIONAL LEARNING
Mindful Teams

What to Do
Point out that you can't learn unless you're mindful and able to focus with deep attention. Have students volunteer some of their unique skills. Choose as team captains two students with skills that are not universal but are teachable with ten minutes' effort. Assign half of the class to each team.

What to Say
We are going to have a friendly mindfulness contest. Your team captains are going to teach you a new skill. It will take everyone's attention and focus to make this happen. Listen to your captains carefully. Notice who needs help and offer it. The team that best demonstrates their new skill will win.

Why It's Important
As they connect mindful awareness and successful learning, students may be surprised to see how much control they have over learning. For some, it may have been an automatic process. For others, it may have been elusive and mysterious. Both will benefit by knowing they can drive the process.

Literature Link
Two-Minute Mysteries

by Donald J. Sobol
(1967). New York: Scholastic.

Nothing takes more mindful awareness than a good mystery, and this book has plenty of them. These short mysteries will take all the focus you've got. Can you pay attention to the important details and solve the puzzle?

Connect this intriguing book to the students' understanding of the role of the PFC in mindful awareness. Point out that jumping to conclusions can work against your sleuthing prowess.

More Books to Share

Gauthier, Gail. (2005). *Happy Kid*. New York: Putnam.

Holbrook, Sara. (1997). *I Never Said I Wasn't Difficult*. Honesdale, PA: Boyds Mills Press.

Thimmesh, Catherine. (2006). *Team Moon*. New York: Houghton Mifflin.

the Optimistic classroom™ library

Focused Awareness: The Core Practice

What Is the Core Practice?

Pause. Listen. Breathe. It can take less than a minute to cue our minds to relax and focus. A short listening and breathing exercise introduced in this lesson—the Core Practice—helps students quiet their minds and get ready to learn.

Why Practice Focused Awareness?

Designed to be used several times a day—especially during transitions when students need help settling down to work or shifting their attention between subjects or tasks—the MindUP Core Practice is the signature daily routine of the MindUP program. The Core Practice puts students in control of their mental and physical energy. By concentrating on the sensations of a resonant sound and then of their own breathing, students calm their minds and get ready to focus on the next part of their day. For the individual student, the Core Practice supports self-regulation and mindful action. For the class community, the Core Practice becomes a time for setting the tone and getting everyone—teacher and students—to achieve a state of mind in which they can all participate purposefully and thoughtfully.

What Can You Expect to Observe?

"My students used to struggle to keep themselves quiet on the outside while bursting from the inside. They would fidget and squirm with the effort of it. Getting quiet on the inside first makes paying attention so much easier for them."
—Sixth-grade teacher

Linking to Brain Research

Controlling Our Breathing

Focusing on breathing helps calm the body by slowing heart rate, lowering blood pressure, and sharpening focus. Paying attention to breathing also supports strong functioning in the higher brain. Controlled breathing lessens anxiety by overriding the "fight, flight, or freeze" response set off by the amygdala and gives control to conscious thought, which takes place in the prefrontal cortex. When breathing is deliberately regulated, the brain is primed to think first and then plan a response, enabling mindful behavior.

Teaching children to focus on and control their breathing can help them become less reactive and more reflective when feeling anxious or stressed. The short daily activity of listening and breathing (Core Practice) introduced in this lesson capitalizes on neuroplasticity, the brain process that creates and strengthens nerve cell (neuron) connections through practice or repeated experience. One example of this growth occurs on the receiving end of the neurons involved in repeated thoughts and actions: Branch-like receptors called dendrites increase in number and size, enabling a more efficient passage of information along frequently used neural pathways. This is one of many ways in which the structure of the brain is flexible and ready to grow.

As children practice controlled breathing, their brains develop and reinforce the "habit" of responding to anxiety by focusing on breathing. This leads to reflective rather than reactive responses. The more controlled breathing is practiced, the more self-managed and mindful children can become.

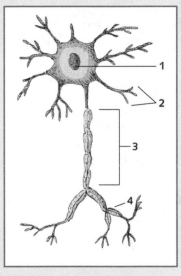

Nerve cells, or neurons, carry messages through electrochemical impulses or signals. The cell body (soma) [1] houses the neuron's control center (nucleus). Dendrites [2] receive information from other neurons. The axon [3] relays the signal from the dendrites to [4] the nerve endings, which transmit the information to other neurons.

Clarify for the Class

Have student use their hand and forearms to show the parts of a neuron: The palm is the nucleus, the fingers are dendrites, the forearm is the axon, and the several sticky flags attached at the elbow are the nerve endings. Show how the information moves from the dendrites through the axon and gets sent along to another neuron's dendrites (students can link up fingers to elbows to create an information path).

Discuss: Think of something you practice a lot. Use your arm-hand model to show one of the neurons in the network before you began practicing and after several practice sessions.

Getting Ready

Taking the Core Practice to Lunch
Common meeting times, such as just after lunch and homeroom period, offer daily opportunities to do the Core Practice.

GOALS
- Students learn an exercise that combines listening and breathing to calm and focus their minds.
- Students discover the importance of practicing focusing exercises regularly.

MATERIALS
- chart paper
- instrument that resonates with a clear, distinctive tone for 10–20 seconds (e.g., triangle, xylophone, chimes, piano, bell, violin)

CREATING THE OPTIMISTIC CLASSROOM
Classroom Management Set norms for mindful practices. Discuss what the Core Practice and other mindful exercises look and sound like when the class is doing them effectively. Elicit students' help in creating a simple T-chart (similar to the one that follows) of reminders on chart paper:

What Mindful Stillness Looks Like	What Mindful Stillness Sounds Like
We look comfortable and at ease.	Our voices are silent.
Our bodies are as still as they can be.	There are no loud noises in the room.
Our eyes are closed or focused downward.	Our breathing is quiet, slow, and relaxed.
Our faces look relaxed.	

Familiar Sound
Using a special sound consistently
to initiate the Core Practice helps
keep students focused and makes
the routine safe and familiar.

MINDUP Warm-Up

Inner and Outer Stillness

Explain to students that they can use their breathing in order to quiet their amygdala and focus their PFCs. Using the following script, guide them through a two-minute exercise. It will help to let them stretch and shake their muscles loose before you begin:

- Sit in a comfortable position and make sure your shoulders are relaxed.
- Relax your jaw. Let your eyelids get heavy. Close your eyes if you wish.
- Notice your breath coming in and going out. Don't try to change it.
- Feel your stomach rising and falling. Let your belly be soft and relaxed.
- Now see if you can breath a little more slowly and a little more deeply.
- If your mind gets distracted, go back to noticing your breath.
- Open your eyes slowly, take a deep breath, and smile.

Discuss: How did this breathing exercise feel? Did your mind quiet down? How hard was it to focus your mind on your breathing?

Leading the Lesson

Practice the Core Practice

Engage	Explore

What to Do

The Core Practice combines a listening exercise like the one in Lesson 2 with the controlled breathing in this lesson's warm-up. Choose an instrument to use for the Core Practice. First, review mindful listening by sounding a note. Encourage students to notice and comment on its resonance and duration.

- We are going to use this sound every time we do our mindful quiet exercise. We will begin with listening to the sound for as long as it lasts.

Ask students to prepare themselves by

- sitting upright and comfortably at their desks, feet flat on the floor (or sitting in a circle on the floor, cross-legged)

- resting their hands comfortably in their laps

- closing their eyes or looking down at their hands

Play a note and let it reverberate. When the sound finally fades, have students open their eyes. Invite their initial reactions. Ask students to be alert to any movements or tension in their body while they listen. Repeat once or twice.

Prepare students for combining mindful listening with mindful breathing to begin the Core Practice. Explain the exercise.

- We will begin our Core Practice by sitting comfortably and closing our eyes or looking down into our hands.

- When you hear the note, listen until it fades away into the quiet. When the sound is gone, begin to focus on every breath.

- When you hear the sound a second time, listen as long as you can, still breathing calmly.

- When you can't hear the sound any longer, slowly open your eyes, but remain still and quiet.

Check that students understand the directions. Then play a note from the instrument. Pause for at least 10 seconds after the sound has stopped, for mindful breathing. Play the note a second time, and observe as students open their eyes.

Why It's Important

The sound when repeated will begin to create an association with quiet focus in their brains. This resonant sound will become a signal for beginning and ending the Core Practice, so it is essential that you **use the same resonant instrument consistently.**

Have students imagine a string pulling up from the crown of the head, with chin pointing down slightly, and spine long. Good posture makes it easier to breathe fully, improves circulation, and supports an alert mind.

Students who are uncomfortable closing their eyes can simply look down at their hands—the point being to avoid visual distractions.

Reflect

Invite students to share their experiences. How many times did they catch their minds wandering? Relate the Core Practice to the key parts of the brain.

- Can you describe the effect that this exercise has on your brain?

Help students understand that although their mind chatter might be hard to control at first, it doesn't matter, as long as they continue to refocus. Their brains will get better at it.

You model aloud how you deal with your own mind chatter during Core Practice. You could do a think-aloud for students so they realize that their efforts are normal: *OK, I'm sitting here listening. The sound is buzzing a little. So is my foot. Uh oh. I think my foot is asleep. I can't shake it now. I'm supposed to sit still. Oh no, how long have I been chattering away in my mind? OK. I'm focusing back on the sound now.*

Announce to the class the scheduled times during the day at which students will be encouraged to practice their new skill. Invite them to practice controlled breathing on their own also, especially if they feel the need to calm their amygdala or focus their PFC.

With practice, students will be able to quiet their minds more quickly and for longer durations. Students who have trouble holding their attention may need to make sure that they are not physically uncomfortable, which can be very distracting.

It is critical to keep a consistent schedule for leading the Core Practice and make sure that students are fully seated and silent before you begin.

MINDUP In the Real World

Career Connection

Listen, aim, focus, breathe, shoot. We can see that the Core Practice helps us every day, no matter what we're doing. One profession that really depends on mindful breathing and listening is that of the wildlife photographer. We owe our most spectacular wildlife photography to the mindful steps the photographer follows before each shot. Sometimes enduring months in remote, challenging environments stalking an elusive animal like the snow leopard, the photographer must listen intently to know when the animal is near and breathe mindfully to ensure a steady hand and an in-focus photograph snapped at exactly the right moment.

Discuss: What other careers require mindful listening and breathing to get centered before a person takes an action? Think about performers and athletes who may need to get focused before they take the stage, court, or field.

Once a Day

Do one minute of mindful breathing or listen to a piece of calming music just prior to a task or part of your day that demands your full concentration and focus.

Connecting to the Curriculum

Learning the Core Practice supports students' connection to their own learning process and to the content areas and literature.

Journal Writing

Encourage your students to reflect on what they've learned about the Core Practice and to record questions to explore at another time. They may enjoy responding to these prompts:

- Draw a cartoon of someone practicing mindful listening and breathing. Show the person sitting quietly with a giant thought bubble overhead. What is in the bubble?

- Make a before-and-after T-chart. Write down how you feel before you practice mindful breathing and afterward. Notice how your body feels and how you mind feels.

- Make a list of some potentially stressful situations that would be helped if you had a minute to practice mindful breathing first. What difference do you think it would make?

- The more comfortable you are, the less distracted you will be when you focus your mind. Draw a diagram that shows the best clothing to wear and position to sit in for practicing mindful breathing and listening.

the Optimistic classroom™ journal

SCIENCE
Practice Neuron Pathways

What to Do

Have students demonstrate how practice forms pathways in the brain. Tell students they are going to line up in alphabetical order so that they can pass an object, such as piece of chalk, from hand to hand. Let them know that their fingers represent dendrites, bringing in information. Their hands represent the neural cell. Their arms represent the axon taking information away.

What to Say

First we'll line up in first-name alphabetical order. Then we'll line up in birthday order. Then we'll try both again. Each attempt will be timed. Are you ready? Line up from A to Z. Let's write down the time. Now line up from January to December. Let's record that time, too. Now, let's see if practice makes a difference when we do it again.

Why It's Important

This modeling of how practice changes the brain will help encourage students who find the Core Practice difficult. By showing them a model of how practice can make big improvements, students may be emboldened to continue through difficulties if they feel confident that they will see results.

LANGUAGE ARTS
Automatic Writing

What to Do

When you're trying to quiet your mind, it seems to want to chatter even more. Set students up with pens and paper and have them write their thoughts as quickly as they can, getting them down on the paper. Tell them this is called automatic writing. It is a great way to begin creative writing.

What to Say

Did you have a hard time controlling your thoughts when you were trying to focus your mind during Core Practice? Well, here is a chance to let your thoughts run wild. Don't try to control them—just write down whatever comes. It might be silly or embarrassing. No one has to see it. If you start to write something interesting, you can save it for another writing assignment.

Why It's Important

This exercise will help students with their Core Practice because it will teach them to notice their thoughts without getting caught up in them. Thoughts will always pop up during mindful listening and breathing. But if students don't stop and focus on them, they will start to quiet down.

HEALTH
Straight-Up Posture

What to Do

Remind students how they practice good posture during Core Practice. When the ears, shoulder, and hips are in a line, the skeletal system takes weight off the muscles. Standing or sitting with good posture also changes your attitude. Good posture makes you more relaxed and more confident. Show students how they can test their posture and correct it.

What to Say

Stand a few inches from a wall. Let your head and body lean against the wall. Your legs won't touch. Stand tall to your full height. Now slide your hand behind your lower back. Keep your palm flat against the wall. If you hand doesn't fit, arch your back a little. If you can fit a fist in the curve, tilt your hips forward a little. Now try and keep that posture as you walk away.

Why It's Important

Good posture is not just important for mindful exercises. Good posture can prevent backaches and even headaches. It also helps maintain good balance. Bad posture puts more pressure on the heart and lung area. Over time, bad posture becomes a habit that is hard to correct.

SOCIAL-EMOTIONAL LEARNING
Mindful Charades

What to Do

Have students generate a list of everyday activities, such as brushing one's teeth or shooting a basketball. Put these ideas on slips of paper to be chosen at random. Ask for two volunteers, one from each team, to do the action—one mindfully and one unmindfully. Let the two decide who will take which approach, then give them 30 seconds to prepare.

What to Say

Form two teams to observe different versions of the same activity. You must guess both the activity and the approach— mindful or unmindful. Watch the two versions, then write down your best guess about the activity and a few adverbs to describe how it was done. The team with the most right answers wins.

Why It's Important

Students have felt the difference that the Core Practice can make. Observing the confidence and grace that come from being relaxed and focused is also motivating, especially to this age group.

Literature Link
The Hunger Games

by Suzanne Collins
(2007). New York: Scholastic.

In a future world where food is scarce and teens must compete for their lives, mindful listening and staying calm are a matter of life and death. Competitors get to play this game only once, and the losers lose it all.

Say: *As you read, notice how characters focus their PFCs and control their amygdala. What happens when they don't?*

More Books to Share

Gallo, Donald, ed. (2007). *What Are You Afraid Of?* New York: Dial Candlewick.

Hipp, Earl (2008). *Fighting Invisible Tigers.* Minnesota: Free Spirit Press.

Johnson, D.B. (2004). *Henry Works.* New York: Houghton Mifflin.

Sharpening Your Senses

By mindfully observing their senses, students will become adept at sharpening their attention and using sensory experiences to enhance memory, problem solving, relationships, creativity, and physical performance.

Expanding on Lessons 2 and 3, students practice honing their skills in focused listening by participating in an auditory awareness activity.

This lesson demonstrates and emphasizes the importance of paying close attention to detail, using visual memory.

Students use their sense of smell to help focus their attention and gain access to key memories and feelings.

Slowing down to focus on the taste of food can completely change a routine activity and make it a mindful, healthy experience.

Comparing and contrasting excited and calm states of the body helps students make important connections between physical sensations and stress levels.

Students learn two balancing postures that foster awareness of how healthy movement practice can improve physical, emotional, and social well-being.

If you can detect a scent of basil as you walk by a restaurant or spot a contact lens that's dropped on a tile floor, your brain is well trained to zero in on important sensory details.

That same ability to notice important details and differentiate among all the scents, sounds, visual images, and other sensory details your brain receives can also help you respond more mindfully to people and events around you.

We know that each time students deliberately focus their attention, as they do in this unit's lessons, they activate their sensory data filter, the reticular activating system, and its pathways to the prefrontal cortex. This repeated stimulation makes the neural circuits stronger.

The practice of focused, mindful awareness enhances the ability of all young learners to direct their attention where it is needed.

Mindful Listening

What Is Mindful Listening?

From the buzz of a cell phone to the wail of a siren, sounds are all around us. Mindful listening helps us choose which sounds to focus our attention on and helps us to be thoughtful in the way we hear and respond to the words of others.

Why Practice Mindful Listening?

Research suggests that students become more focused and responsive to their environment by participating in mindful listening activities, such as Audio Alert in this lesson. In fact, training our brains to concentrate on specific sounds helps heighten our sensory awareness. As students monitor their own auditory experience—noting what they choose to focus on and/or respond to—they build self-awareness and self-management skills. Mindful listening also lays the groundwork for social awareness and effective communication—an important part of the Common Core Standards.

Being able to listen in a focused way to what others say and to home in on details such as tone and inflection gives a listener a clearer notion about the meaning of the words and a better idea for how to respond. This work helps prepare students for following directions, resolving conflicts through discussion, building friendships, and listening critically to news, ads, and other media messages.

What Can You Expect to Observe?

"Students really make an effort tune in to details of the sounds they hear and point out the nuances of sounds that make them distinct. They'll apply mindful listening to observing the way people speak to one another—in particular, identifying the tone of someone's voice and monitoring their own."

—Eighth-grade teacher

Linking to Brain Research

What Is the RAS?

An intricate network of long nerve pathways lies within the core of the brain stem. This reticular formation, also called the reticular activating system (RAS), helps regulate many basic body functions and connects the brain stem to the prefrontal cortex (PFC) and other parts of the brain. The RAS helps keep the brain awake and alert and is the brain's attention-focusing center. Sensory stimuli (visual, auditory, tactile, olfactory, taste) continually arrive via the spinal cord and are sorted and screened by the RAS. The sensory input deemed relevant by the RAS is routed on to its appropriate destination in the conscious brain. What's irrelevant is blocked.

The RAS is critically important because the brain cannot process the millions of bits of sensory information coming in at once! A student sitting in a classroom likely has competing sensory experiences—the voice of her teacher, the vibration of a cell phone, the sight of a friend walking by the classroom, the aroma of food from the cafeteria. It's easy to imagine how these stimuli might cause her to shift her attention from the classroom to what she hopes to eat for lunch. A mindful, focused student is able to reassure herself that lunch period will come after math and to redirect her attention to the task at hand.

Athletes, musicians, scholars, and other "focused" people have "trained" their RAS to choose the most pertinent sensory stimuli. With practice focusing on specific details, students can train their RAS to be more effective. Such practice is especially important for students who have trouble focusing their attention on their work, instructions, or social cues. Sensory awareness activities in this lesson and the others in this unit provide your students with repeated RAS-strengthening practice.

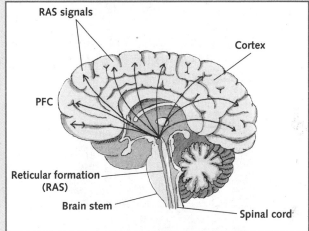

The RAS serves as an "executive personal secretary" to the PFC, forwarding on only what's immediately relevant.

Clarify for the Class

Make a model of the RAS using a kitchen strainer, fine sand, and gravel. Demonstrate how a strainer allows only some things to pass through. Similarly, the RAS holds back unimportant sensory input, but lets relevant information pass on to the PFC.

Discuss: What kinds of sensory input do you think are filtered out by the RAS? (background noise, feeling clothes on body, smell of your own home, etc.) Give examples of situations where you noticed these things. What did you think was happening in your brain at those times?

Getting Ready

Listen Up!
Students record descriptions of sounds they heard during the Audio Alert lesson.

GOALS
- Students train their attention on specific sounds and try to identify those sounds.
- Students learn how mindful listening skills can help them communicate more successfully.

MATERIALS
- various common objects for creating sounds or a set of sound effects downloaded from the Internet (search for "free sound effects")
- Audio Alert/Present Scent activity sheet (p. 154)

CREATING THE OPTIMISTIC CLASSROOM
Classroom Management Tell students, "The tone of your voice can say as much as the words you speak." Ask students if they can detect the mood of a friend, family member, or teacher by carefully listening to the tone of that person's voice. Help them understand that the tone we use gives our words an emotional charge that can strengthen or hurt our relationships. Encourage students to be mindful of the way they communicate their feelings through speech. Pair up students and have them practice modulating their tone in three different ways using the phrase "I can't talk right now" and then discuss the feelings each tone conveyed.

Tuned in to Learning
Having students create a file
of free online sound effects
is a great way to incorporate
technology into this mindful
listening lesson.

MINDUP Warm-Up

Mindful Listening Practice

Build background for this lesson with an auditory-kinesthetic rhythm exercise. Give students a rhythmic clapping and snapping pattern to follow (e.g., clap, clap, snap, clap, snap, clap). Call on students to create their own easy rhythms (three to five beats), then ask them to try increasingly challenging patterns (six to eight beats).

When students are able to come up with unique patterns and repeat the patterns of their peers, organize the class in groups of six to ten and have them play a rhythmic listening game, seated in a circle. Give each group a basic pattern or have the group come up with its own. One at a time, students present a variation on the basic pattern and repeat their new version, cuing the group to repeat their pattern the third time. Suggestions:

- Limit the variations to six or eight beats to avoid too much complexity.
- Model how to make the variation rhythmically interesting by dividing or omitting beats, for example.
- In between turns, encourage the group to return to the original pattern, so it remains fresh in students' minds.

Discuss: What did you have to do in order to keep track of the pattern? How is this kind of listening similar to or different from the kind of listening you do in class? in conversations with friends?

Leading the Lesson

Audio Alert

Engage	Explore

What to Do

Engage

Review mindfulness and the parts of the brain from Unit 1, as needed. Initiate a discussion about listening.

- Let's consider why listening is important—for school, for friendships & family, for pleasure (music) and for safety.

- Do you think listening is a skill or a talent? What might be the difference?

- When there's lots of noise around you, what do you do to help you pay attention to just one sound, like a friend's voice on a cell-phone call? What are some times when you are able to eliminate distractions and focus on a single important sound?

Explain that together, the class will participate in an inquiry experience that will help students develop mindful listening.

Explore

Ask students to close their eyes and sit comfortably while you, or a chosen student, either stand out of sight with objects or cue up sound effects you've downloaded.

- Listen as mindfully as you can to the sound I make—and focus on it. If you think you know what it is, record your answer on the Audio Alert Activity Sheet.

One at a time, make each sound. Possible actions:
–drop a hardcover book on a counter top.
–shuffle a deck of cards
–set off a vibrating cell phone ring tone
(Sound effects online may include a skateboard coasting, a waterfall, or the rattle of a roller coaster.)

Give students time to record their answers on the Audio Alert activity sheet. Encourage them to include specific descriptions of each sound—noting that each sound may include more than one distinct sound.

When the listening exercise is complete, allow students to share their descriptions and predictions. Then reveal the identity of the sound-makers.

Why It's Important

Engage

There are many sounds surrounding us most of the time. Usually we aren't mindful of every sound, because our brain helps us focus our attention by screening the sounds our ears pick up and bringing to our attention only the ones that are important. That filter in our brain is the Reticular Activating System (RAS). Listening mindfully can help us reinforce the work of the RAS.

Explore

By concentrating on specific sounds, you can train your RAS to listen very carefully. That strengthens the pathways to the prefrontal cortex—so you can get the information you're listening for more efficiently.

You are more in control of your own thought processes if you are more aware of the constant sensory input that your brain experiences.

Reflect

Initiate a class discussion. Make sure students understand that they were using brain energy to identify each sound and to concentrate on the distinct parts of each sound.

- In what ways is this experience different from the way we typically listen to sounds? If you lost your focus on the sounds, explain what you think got in the way.

- How might this kind of listening affect your brain?

- How was trying to identify sounds good practice for mindful listening?

Record student responses on chart paper.

When you're really listening well, you get the information you need without being distracted. Then you can decide how best to respond.

MINDUP
In the Real World

Career Connection

Is mindful listening ever a matter of life and death? Sometimes YES! Every day, doctors practice mindful listening on the job. Not only do they need to listen carefully to their patients' bodies—hearts, lungs, and abdomens—but also to the patients themselves. What brings the patient to the doctor? What symptoms is he or she experiencing? Doctors work hard to learn the skill of active, attentive listening. Once the patient's medical history is recorded, the doctor can ask informed questions and order the right tests that will lead to the correct diagnosis and effective treatment. In the hospital, mindful listening saves people's lives.

Discuss with students how this and other careers depend on mindful listening. Examples include 911 operators, customer service representatives, and guidance counselors.

Once a Day

Resist the urge to immediately answer a question from a student or colleague. Savor the time to reflect and develop a thoughtful response.

Connecting to the Curriculum

Mindful listening supports students' observation of their own learning processes and promotes awareness in the content areas and in literature.

Journal Writing

Encourage your kids to reflect on what they've learned about mindful listening and to record questions to explore at another time. They may also enjoy responding to these prompts:

- Use a T-chart to show the differences between mindful listening and everyday listening.

- Pick a word or a phrase and mindfully listen for the word or phrase during lunch. Explain why you think you did or did not hear the word or phrase during lunch with your friends.

- Select a class or an activity during which you have difficulty concentrating. Determine to listen mindfully for one class period or during one activity. What did you do to stay focused? Describe your experience.

- Tell about a time when being a mindful listener helped you or someone else in a difficult or dangerous situation.

SCIENCE & HEALTH
Protect Your Hearing!

What to Do
If your school owns or can borrow a decibel meter, have students take decibel measures and create a chart of school sounds, such as slamming lockers in the hall between classes, cafeteria or gym noise, and so on. If you are unable to locate a decibel meter, have students create a "meter" of their own. The fire alarm bell could represent the loudest sound, while the closing of a paperback book could be the softest. Have students chart school sounds between these two extremes. Check out excellent graphics and a video at www.dangerousdecibels.org/hearingloss.cfm.

What to Say
As we've been learning, we're surrounded by sounds and some of these can really hurt our ears—permanently. Damage to the sensitive hair cells in our ears can be done by the loudness or pressure of something we hear. For example, a typical conversation is 60 dB—not enough to cause damage. But listening to music on your earbuds at a high volume (100 dB) for even 15 minutes a day can cause permanent damage in a short period of time.

Why It's Important
Doing an activity to heighten students' awareness of the dangers of noise will encourage them to value and protect their hearing.

LANGUAGE ARTS
What Sounds Similar in These Expressions?

What to Do
Have students share a common phrase in several different languages and listen closely to compare the versions. Encourage students to use the second language they are studying or a home language other than English. You may also want to have students write the phrases and compare the written versions. You may be able to identify similar word roots.

What to Say
How do you say "Good morning" in the second language you're studying or in a language you know other than English? . . . Let's listen to the sounds of each and notice if there are any similarities among these expressions. What's unique about each one? Let's take a closer look at the phrases by writing them on the board.

Why It's Important
Comparing common phrases in several languages helps broaden students' understanding of language structure, knowlege of the world, and awareness of cultural similarities and uniqueness.

LANGUAGE ARTS
Sounds Remembered

What to Do

Ask students to copy the following list and write the sounds they associate with each word. Allow students to add to the list.

calm	anger	excite
comfort	agitate	entertain

Model how to use the sounds with the words to write a 5-line poem focused on mood and sound. For example, for "anger," students may suggest *cry, shout, yell, scream, slam.*

What to Say

What sounds come to mind when you feel calm? How about angry? Are they sounds from a certain experience you've had in a specific place? . . . Let's gather some more sound details. Close your eyes and imagine yourself in the scene you pictured for one of the words on the list. What are you hearing? Make a list or word web to record the sound words and descriptions. . . . Now let's put those ideas together in a powerful way in five short descriptive lines.

Why It's Important

Sounds are often linked to strong emotions, and in writing, well-used sound words can give immediacy to emotions. Using mindful listening as a tool for elaboration can help create moments of emotional intensity in descriptive and narrative writing.

SOCIAL-EMOTIONAL LEARNING
To Interview Is to Listen Well

What to Do

Have students prepare to interview an important adult in their lives, such as a grandparent or coach. Have them write out three or four questions about that person's life (e.g., What was your most challenging decision as a teenager? What is your favorite childhood memory?). Review pointers about how to listen well. Set a time for students to share what they learned by paraphrasing the most interesting part of the interview. Then have them write down the key idea or event and tell why that resonated most.

What to Say

Important people in our lives can often tell us stories about the life experiences that helped shape who they are. Let's discuss how to ask questions that will help you get interesting and informative answers—and how to be an excellent listener.

Why It's Important

A thoughtful question is a tool to help us listen mindfully. Listening and reflecting on others' life experiences can help us decide how to act mindfully in similar situations.

Literature Link
The Raven and Other Poems

by Edgar Allan Poe
(2000). New York: Scholastic.

Edgar Allan Poe, a classic wordsmith, used rhythm and other sound elements to elicit emotion. Invite students to read aloud these classic poems and listen to the way the word choice and rhythm create a spooky, chilling mood. These poems can serve as a counterpoint to other poems students have read that elicit very different moods and emotions.

Connect this book to attentiveness, auditory discrimination skills, creative expression through writing, and understanding what another person is trying to communicate.

More Books to Share

Adoff, Jaime. (2002). *Song Shoots Out of My Mouth: A Celebration of Music.* New York: Dutton Juvenile.

Creech, Sharon. (2001). *Love That Dog.* New York: HarperCollins.

Miller, Sarah. (2007). *Miss Spitfire: Reaching Helen Keller.* New York: Simon & Schuster.

Mindful
Seeing

What is Mindful Seeing?
Crimson or ruby? Ovoid or oblong? Smile or smirk? Our ability to visually distinguish precise details has given rise to a very rich and precise descriptive vocabulary. Mindful seeing enables us to better observe ourselves, other people, and our surroundings to more fully enjoy and learn from them.

Why Practice Mindful Seeing?
As with mindful listening, mindful seeing helps students sharpen their focus by calling on one sense to very purposefully observe an object. This lesson also takes advantage of students' natural visual curiosity about important people and things in their environment—and their desire to share their observations.

As they practice mindful seeing exercises, students become increasingly attuned to observing details by slowing down and focusing their attention. We can build on these skills of observation by encouraging students to apply their curiosity and perceptiveness to their academic work. In fact, sharpening visual discrimination skills can help improve skills critical in almost any subject area, whether students are making careful observations during science labs or visualizing descriptions in a literary work. And in the area of social-emotional learning, these skills can be tied to reading social cues and acting perceptively in response to the facial expressions and body language of others.

What Can You Expect to Observe?
"Students would take for granted that they had seen everything just by looking around casually. They were shocked to learn how many details they were missing. Now when I have them look at an image or diagram mindfully, they really notice what's in front of them."

—Seventh-grade teacher

Linking to Brain Research

Emotions Shape Behavior and Learning

The amygdala, that reactive watchdog of the brain, elicits the same fear response for perceived danger as for genuine danger. The behavior of a child who feels unsafe, threatened, inadequate, judged, or vulnerable to ridicule is driven by his or her brain's reaction to threat. Children who feel continually "on alert" are unable to engage in mindful behavior because their amygdala blocks incoming stimuli from reaching the rational prefrontal cortex.

The brain gives priority to emotions because they matter. Emotions are associated with the places and people in children's lives. Children who learn to associate school with a feeling of safety become confident enough to move out of their comfort zone. They feel safe expressing their ideas, working together, asking questions, and trying new things—even if it means making mistakes. You might say they train their amygdala to remain calm, keeping the information pathways to their higher brain open at school. And the more a child feels safe at school, the stronger those neural pathways become. The chains of neurons that result in a feeling of safety become more efficient, passing the message along faster.

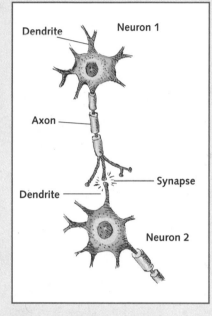

Neurons connect axon to dendrite, passing messages along via gap-jumping electrochemical exchanges called synapses.

Clarify for the Class

Model how chains of neurons pass messages and that neural pathways get faster and stronger with use and repetition. Review the parts of a nerve cell (see page 43) and explain that everyone is going to be a neuron: left hands are dendrites, which receive messages; torsos are the cell bodies; right arms are message-shuttling axons; right hands are the nerve endings and transfer messages to the next neuron's dendrites (left hand). Choose a "message" to pass, such as a coin, eraser or pebble. Using a stopwatch or clock, time the lined-up chain of "neurons" as the first message passes from nerve ending (right hand) to a dendrite (left hand) of the adjacent to a nerve ending (right hand) of the next and so on until the message is received by the final neuron. Then repeat a number of times, recording seconds elapsed.

Discuss: Did the message travel faster with practice? How much faster each time? How is that like what happens in the brain?

Getting Ready

Choose a Specimen
A student selects a specimen to examine.

GOALS
- Students practice focusing their attention on an object and describe the visual details they observe.
- Students strengthen their visual vocabulary and memory through mindful seeing.

MATERIALS
- enough similar objects so that each student has something to examine (coins, glass beads, tree leaves, puzzle pieces, or other objects that are similar but have noticeable distinguishing details)
- (optional) Sensory Web activity sheet (p. 155)

CREATING THE OPTIMISTIC CLASSROOM
Supporting English Language Learners Making ELLs feel welcome and safe to participate among fluent English speakers is critical for helping them prime their brains for learning. Suggest that ELLs brainstorm words for their descriptions in their first language. Make online language dictionaries available and show students how to use them to translate to and from English. Remind them to be on the lookout for cognates, words that are similar in meaning and spelling across the languages. Cognates give their English vocabulary a head start.

Compare and Contrast
Comparing and contrasting
specimens helps build skills of
analysis and discrimination.

MINDUP Warm-Up

Description Building

Help students expand their vocabulary to describe the things they notice accurately
and precisely. Find display images from online sites that use color, line, texture, shape,
and other key visual elements very differently (e.g., images by Grandma Moses,
Matisse, and Kandinsky).

Ask students how each artist described his or her subject. Guide them to describe
colors more precisely (bright or dark, bold or soft, clear or muddy, introduce names
for colors that students may not be familiar with: teal, vermillion, mauve, chartreuse,
indigo), line quality (long, straight, thick, thin, curvy, angular), shapes (soft- or
hard-edged, distinct or blurry, two or three dimensional), and size of objects. Invite
students to record new vocabulary words in their journals.

Discuss: Set up a Venn diagram (add rings as necessary) in order to compare and
contrast the images. Are there any words that overlap? Which are unique?

Leading the Lesson

Similar, Not the Same

Engage

Explore

What to Do

Review terms students have generated from the Warm-Up and connect accurate description to mindful seeing. Introduce the concept of a specimen and set the lesson goal.

- Using mindful seeing skills is important in many subject areas—for visualizing shapes in geometry, or classifying species in biology, for example.

- The objects that scientists study—like fossils for paleontologists and unusual insects for entomologists—are called specimens. Have you ever found a piece of something and tried to figure out what it was?

- Today you're going to examine some specimens so closely that each of you will be able to pick out the one you've studied from a group of specimens that looks almost exactly the same.

Organize students in groups of five or six. (The more students are in the group, the more challenging the activity is.) Distribute the specimens.

- When you get your specimen, be very quiet and focus all of your attention on it. Let your PFC note every little detail, and let your RAS pass along all the images it can.

Ask students to hold the specimen in the palm of their hand and observe it from all sides. Prompt them to notice qualities like color, shape, and size, and to notice any imperfections or unique details. Make sure they have at least a minute of complete silence with their specimen. Encourage them to take notes on a blank piece of paper or use the Sensory Web page to record the visual features they notice.

For each group, gather the specimens in a box, mix them up, hand the box back to the group and invite students to find their original specimen by comparing and contrasting those in the set. If there is any dispute, have the group repeat the exercise until each student has found his or her specimen.

Why It's Important

Powers of observation are valuable in many curriculum areas and help establish an inquisitive mind-set. Setting students in the role of scientist helps to provide them with a real-world context for mindful seeing. This also builds a foundational skill in science and can be repeated or recalled any time you plan to teach a lesson or plan an experiment that requires visual observation.

Using prompts can guide students to notice important details they may not have noticed otherwise. This is a useful activity to repeat, especially if students don't notice many details the first time—as with other mindful awareness activities, building visual observation skills takes practice.

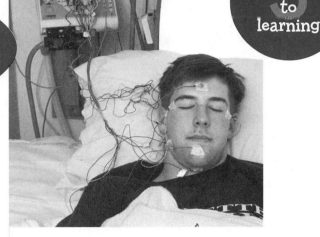

Reflect

Have the groups relate any difficulties they had identifying their specimens. Discuss the way they were focused and how that helped them notice those details.

- Which details helped you identify your specimen?

- How much effort did this kind of seeing take, compared to the usual way of looking at things?

Compare mindful seeing to the mindful listening activity.

- How was mindful seeing with your specimens similar to mindful listening to the mystery sounds? Which was easier for you?

Have students consider how mindful seeing helps them (or could help them) in different situations.

- Think about how mindful seeing might help someone witnessing a crime. How could mindful seeing help someone who wanted to be a sportscaster?

Encourage students to apply some of the visual observation skills and descriptive skills they've worked with in this lesson. Have students consider how they can benefit from mindful seeing in daily life. You may need to help them generate ideas, using examples from your experience (e.g., finding the correct position of a puzzle piece in a jigsaw puzzle or recognizing whether a baseball pitch is a ball or strike).

MINDUP
In the Real World

Career Connection

What do waves have to do with sleep? If you're a sleep technologist—everything! By monitoring instruments that measure a sleeping patient's brain, eye movements, muscle activity, and heart rhythm, the technologist charts sleep stages and identifies problems that may affect a person's sleep. Technologists receive input from 12 different channels and 22 wire attachments to the patient. While keeping an eye on the patients, technologists must also continuously monitor an array of electronic equipment. Only an experienced technologist is able to read and interpret the wave patterns on the screen.

Discuss: Consider the visual focus required of a sports referee, astronomer, or graphic designer. Would you find this kind of mindful seeing enjoyable? Why, or why not?

Once a Day

Choose two similar assignments to scrutinize, such as prewriting exercises done several days apart. Use mindful seeing to observe areas of growth. Review with students what you've noticed so they can build on these improvements.

Connecting to the Curriculum

Mindful seeing supports students' connection to their own learning process and to the content areas and literature.

Journal Writing

Encourage your students to reflect on what they've learned about mindful seeing and to record questions to explore at another time. They may also enjoy responding to these prompts:

- Choose a new vocabulary word from all the words you used in your describing exercises. Write a definition of the word. Draw a picture to help you remember it. Then write an example and a non-example.

- Find a baby picture of yourself or someone you know. Study the picture and find ways to compare and contrast the younger self with the older self. What has stayed the same? What has changed?

- Find a picture of an outfit that has a style you admire. Describe what you see. Sketch a picture to go with your description, if you like. Then describe what you are wearing now. How do the two outfits compare?

- Look for a picture or work of art that you like, and make a frame for it. Fill in the frame with words. Think about the vocabulary that you learned to describe color, lines, and details.

SCIENCE
Eye Am Not Alone

What to Do
Have students go online or use the library to collect resources on the human eye. In pairs, have students create a diagram that explains how the eye works. Then have pairs join up with up other pairs, and add any new details to their diagrams.

What to Say
When you made your diagram of the eye, how complete was it? Give your diagram a +1 for every detail that another pair copied from you. Give your diagram a –1 for every detail you copied. How do the scores on your diagrams compare?

Why It's Important
Making the process of mindful seeing one that invites repeated attempts at observation and that teaches students that careful study can be improved by collaboration (sharing new ways of seeing with peers), by looking closely more than once, and by what they've recorded.

MATH
Partner Puzzles

What to Do
Explain that tangram puzzles are an ancient Chinese game using geometric shapes. Provide a tangram pattern (easily found online) to students. Give students time to cut out the shapes and manipulate them to make different objects. Let students know that they will make puzzles for their classmates to solve.

What to Say
There are many different puzzle shapes you can make with your tangram. You can make animals, such as rabbits and bats, objects, such as candles and sailboats, or people. Make a puzzle shape and trace it twice. Leave the first puzzle empty inside. With the second, make an answer key that shows how you put the tangram pieces together. Then title your puzzle and swap with a partner.

Why It's Important
Turning spatial awareness skills into a puzzle is a fun way to help store information about geometric shapes in the hippocampus, especially for students who are intimidated by math.

the Optimistic™ classroom journal

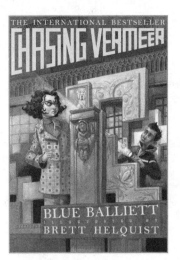

THE INTERNATIONAL BESTSELLER
CHASING VERMEER
BLUE BALLIETT
ILLUSTRATED BY
BRETT HELQUIST

LANGUAGE ARTS
Described to a T

What to Do

Explain that the job of an author is to paint a mental picture using words. This is especially true for a story's setting. Have students choose a favorite novel or short story. If they don't have something in mind, they can choose whatever they are reading for class. If you wish, prepare an excerpt to get them started. Review the excerpt together for descriptive details.

What to Say

Make a T-chart on a piece of paper. On one side write the details you found in the story. Probably not a complete picture, but enough to get your mind working. Use the other side of the T-chart to fill in information from your imagination. Try to picture the scene as if you were really looking at it. How many details can you add? Invite students to compare charts with anyone who wrote about the same book.

Why It's Important

Students will be better readers and they will enjoy it more if they can bring mindful seeing skills to their mind's eye. In this activity they apply the mindful seeing skills they used with everyday objects to what they see in their imagination as they read. Although some students do this naturally, some may have never taken this interactive approach to reading.

SOCIAL-EMOTIONAL LEARNING
Seeing May Not Be Believing

What to Do

Show students an example of an optical illusion. Discuss how the illusion was created. Explain that seeing is often the brain interpreting information. Those interpretations can be played with to make optical illusions.

What to Say

Work with a partner and hunt for optical illusions. What is the coolest one you can find? Copy it and take note of where you found it. Let's make a gallery of optical illusions and share what we've found. Then we can vote for the trickiest one.

Why It's Important

It is important for students to understand that mindful seeing has an interpretative component. What they see may not be as "real" as it seems. This may also help students understand why two people who look at the same thing, may come away with different interpretations.

Literature Link
Chasing Vermeer

by Blue Balliett
(2004). New York: Scholastic.

Students may enjoy trying to solve this mystery that is full of codes and illustrations that hold clues. The story begins when three mysterious letters show up and are linked to the theft of a famous painting by Vermeer. A series of coincidences lead two classmates to get on the case.

Connect this book to exercising mindful seeing because in this story every detail is a potential clue to solving the mystery.

More Books to Share

Raczka, Bob. (2005). *Unlikely Pairs: Fun with Famous Works of Art*. Minneapolis, MN: Millbrook Press.

Seder, Rufus Butler. (2008). *Swing!* New York: Workman Publishing Company.

Shusterman, Neal. (2009). *The Eyes of Kid Midas*. New York: Simon and Schuster.

the Optimistic classroom™ library

Mindful
Smelling

What is Mindful Smelling?

Just by catching a whiff of a familiar scent, our brain can call to mind the people, places, or things we associate with it. Mindful smelling—using our sense of smell to be more aware of our environment—can help us to keenly observe our world and sharpen our memory.

Why Practice Mindful Smelling?

Practicing focused awareness with a new sense, smell, continues to broaden students' ability to observe and enjoy their experiences. As they slow down to study and take notes on several distinct aromas during this lesson, students expand their ability to take in new information without jumping too quickly to judgment—deciding, for example, that a smell is "gross" without further consideration.

By prompting them to stay with their observations, we give students an opportunity to be fully engaged in what they're doing and to reflect on their experiences, which bolsters their sense of self-awareness and self-control. In this lesson, students also discover how memories and important information can be attached to and triggered by smells, because the smell and memory centers in the brain are close to each other.

What Can You Expect to Observe?

"My students were skeptical at first about the strong link between scent and memory. But as we explored this, they began to make connections to their own lives. We found that the smell of a barbecue grill, a pine tree, a certain shampoo, for example, were all connected to moods and memories. And now we're exploring how to harness that power for learning."

—Sixth-grade teacher

Linking to Brain Research

Dopamine: The Chemistry of Pleasure and Reward

Our brains have more than four dozen types of neurotransmitters, chemicals that allow signals to pass between neurons. One of these neurotransmitters, dopamine, plays a role in producing and regulating positive feelings such as pleasure, hopefulness, optimism, and keen interest. When we have sufficient levels of this "feel-good" neurotransmitter in our brain, we are more able to maintain motivation, delay gratification, and feel rewarded and content. As levels of dopamine in the brain change, so does our outlook on life.

Dopamine release is triggered during pleasure-inducing experiences including smelling and eating a favorite food, seeing friends, enjoying sports, solving a puzzle, and accomplishing a task. Studies show that students who learn at a young age to connect the "feel-good" times with positive behaviors are better able to access the self-soothing, internal reward system that comes as standard equipment in every human brain. As those students mature, they are less likely to seek the dopamine surges that come with high-risk behaviors like drugs, alcohol, promiscuity, reckless driving, and overeating. In fact, young people who consistently feel pleasure and reward during sports, music, theater, dance, art, social interaction, and positive classroom experiences are not as likely to be involved in risky behaviors.

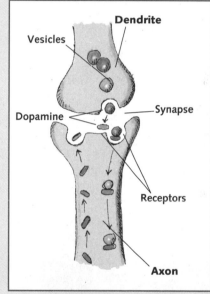

When a dopamine release is triggered, vesicles in the dendrites empty their dopamine and receptors in the axon of the receiving cell are activated to pass the message forward, across the synapse.

Clarify for the Class

Explain that the neurotransmitter dopamine affects the brain's ability to create the positive feelings necessary to concentrate, pay attention, remember, and keep trying—all critical to learning. On the other hand, a lack of dopamine makes people more likely to "self-medicate" with unhealthy behaviors, such as taking drugs, which deplete dopamine even more and create a vicious cycle. Keeping natural dopamine levels high makes us less vulnerable to risky behaviors. Suggest some ways that people can boost dopamine, such as playing sports or games, creating art or music, talking to friends, and learning a new skill.

Discuss: What are some activities you find both fun and rewarding? Can you give an example of a time when you felt better after doing one of these activities? How do you think the level of dopamine in your brain changed during the activity?

Getting Ready

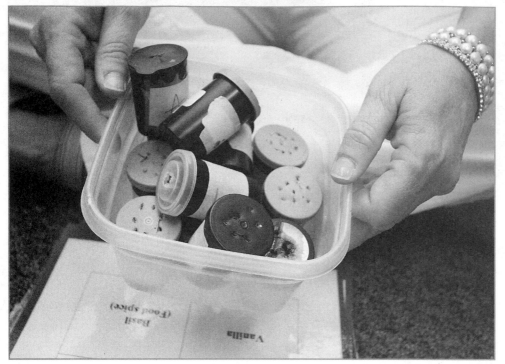

Sorting Scents
Film canisters can be labeled and paired with a sorting sheet to help students classify their scents.

GOALS
- Students focus attention through their sense of smell and describe observations.
- Students identify thoughts and feelings triggered by various scents.

MATERIALS
- chart paper
- 4 sets of small opaque containers with lids, such as film canisters
- 4–5 familiar scents (coffee beans, vinegar, lemon juice, vanilla, cinnamon, ginger, baby powder, peppermint) (NOTE: Check first for food allergies.)
- scratch paper or Audio Alert/Present Scent activity sheet (p. 154)
- Place the scent samples in containers (for liquid scents, use saturated cotton balls). Label each container on the bottom. Create a reference key.

CREATING THE OPTIMISTIC CLASSROOM
Classroom Management During this lesson you may have to remind students to be respectful of each other. Students of this age group are going through many physical changes, and they are fascinated with bodily functions, including body odors and passing gas. They may be experimenting with scents to make themselves more attractive in a somewhat heavy-handed way. Furthermore, there may be a need for cultural sensitivity. Strong cooking spices can change the scent of the body's perspiration. Make sure that the class understands that all mindful exercises include the idea of being mindful of other people's feelings.

Making Sense of Scents
Students discuss the differences
they notice between two scents.

MINDUP Warm-Up

Common Scents

Help students understand that their sense of smell is connected to the amygdala and
the hippocampus. That's why scents can change your mood or bring back memories.
Invite students to list some smells they strongly like or dislike. Students may think of
foods (cookies baking, liver frying) as well as other scents (mowed grass, gasoline).
Choose several popular examples to discuss as a group. For each, ask, "How would
you describe this scent? What memories or moods come to mind when you think of
this scent?"

As with other mindful exercises, encourage students to use descriptions rather than
judgments (e.g., "disgusting" or "amazing"). To help them precisely describe specific
smells, build on chart paper a vocabulary list of descriptive terms they volunteer (or
you introduce), such as *sweet, strong, fresh, mild, pungent, aromatic, rotten, minty,
fruity, spicy, sour, floral, fishy,* and *moldy*.

Discuss: How do you think you could use scents to change your mood?
Which scents would make you feel relaxed? If we could find a scent that was
relaxing, how could that help us remember information we need to know in class?

Leading the Lesson

Present Scent

Engage

Explore

What to Do

Build background for the lesson by making connections to previous mindful sensing exercises.

Point out to students how much sensory information is available through their sense of smell alone. Have them think about the scents they are exposed to every day. You may want to refer to the scent descriptions chart from the Warm-Up as they offer new descriptions.

Let's list smells we've been exposed to so far today:

- What kind of scents did you experience while getting ready for school? What scents do your soap, shampoo, toothpaste have?

- What about the smell of breakfast? lunch?

- What smells did you encounter on the way to school? Was there car exhaust? Did you pass by a coffee shop? What about the classroom smells?

- Does anyone smell a freshly sharpened pencil? Do textbooks have an odor?

Organize the class into four groups, and distribute the first scent to each group. Be sure each group member has a few moments to experience the scent and reflect on it. Ask other group members to keep silent as the scent is passed around.

Use these prompts to help students take notes on scratch paper or record their ideas on the Audio Alert/Present Scent activity sheet.

- What kind of mood or place does this scent make you think of?

- What words best describe this scent?

- What do you think the scent is?

Allow a moment for students to discuss their impressions as a group. This pause will help keep students' olfactory nerves from being overwhelmed. Then pass around the second scent container.

Follow the same procedure for each set of scents.

Why It's Important

As with mindful listening and seeing exercises, concentrating on using a single sense to identify details helps students prime their RAS to gather lots of information from their environments that they might not have otherwise noticed. Taking an account of the smells around them gets them focused on taking cues from their nose—signals they may not be used to noticing.

Explain to students that some of the scents may be pleasant and others less so. Remind them to take in the information without making judgments that influence their group members. Be clear that your expectations include no words, sounds, gestures, or exaggerated facial expressions in reaction to the scent while it's being passed around. Reactions can be shared during the discussion.

Reflect

Circulate each scent sample again as you invite students to share with the class the notes they took on the scent.

- In the warm-up activity, you described scents that you know well and could remember. How was this exercise different? Which activity was more challenging? Why do you think that is?

- Where does the brain store our scent memories? Can you explain why animals and humans might depend on accurate scent memories for survival?

Help students see mindful smelling as a focusing tool.

- Think about how scent can focus the mind and calm down the amygdala when it is overreacting. What are some times during the day that you might pause, close your eyes, and take a moment to smell mindfully to calm and focus?

Encourage students to find a scent that they find calming and use for mindful smelling when they want to relax and focus. They might choose a drop of perfume or cologne on a cotton ball, or a spice, tied in a small piece of cloth. Learning to use the sense of smell more actively and to better understand its role in how the brain functions.

MINDUP
In the Real World

Career Connection

Do you have a nose for rocks? If you have a keen sense of smell, your nose may lead you to a career in geology. Geologists identify rocks and minerals by relying on a range of sensory input that sometimes includes smell. That's because certain rocks and minerals have a distinct odor. Sniffing a rock and breathing deeply and mindfully can help geologists detect, for example, sulfur (smells like rotten eggs), shale (smells like mud), and arsenic (smells like garlic). In fact, Japanese scientists are researching the smell of the moon—in this way they hope to identify the minerals that make up the moon's surface.

Discuss: Think of several types of products you've bought or seen advertised recently. How did marketers use an actual scent or suggest a scent to sell the product? (Consider soaps and beauty products, restaurants, types of food, and holiday items.)

Once a Day

Add a mindful smelling cue to students' Core Practice, such as, "As you breathe in, be aware of classroom scents in the air around you."

Connecting to the Curriculum

Mindful smelling supports students' connection to their own learning process and to the content areas and literature.

Journal Writing

Encourage your students to reflect on what they've learned about mindful smelling and to record questions to explore at another time. They may enjoy responding to these prompts:

- Make a calendar of smells. Go through the seasons and holidays and think of the smells associated with each. Which are your favorites?

- Describe your signature scent. Do you have a favorite fragrance that you like to wear? How about the smell of your soap or shampoo? What would you like your personal scent to communicate about you?

- Keep a scent diary for a week. At the end of each day take a few moments to think about the different scents you noticed that day. Do your best to describe them accurately. Are you noticing and describing smells more clearly by the end of the week?

- Write about your favorite bad smell. It could be something stinky like your dog's breath that you like because you associate it with feelings for your dog. It could be a locker room smell that reminds you of playing your favorite sport. Describe the smell and why you like it.

SCIENCE
Does the Nose Know?

What to Do
Explain to students that our sense of smell has been important to our survival. It helps us know when something is rotten and should not be eaten. Let students try an experiment to see how well the nose can distinguish between edible and inedible objects. Gather clean plastic containers with lids or make lids with aluminum foil and a rubber band. Have students work with a small group.

What to Say
Do you think you can tell by smell if something is good to eat? Work with a group to collect items that you use for your test. Include a mixture of food and nonfood items. (Examples of nonfood items: pine needles, pencil shavings, dirt, soap) Caution students against using anything unsanitary. Label the containers with a key and make a survey sheet for your classmates. How will you present your results?

Why It's Important
Although, the role of smell is reduced today because most of our food is selected from stores or restaurants rather than foraged or harvested by us, this activity shows the important role our sense of smell once played in keeping us alive (enjoying food smells to stimulate appetite) and healthy (e.g., learning to distinguish edible food from spoiled food and nonfood).

SOCIAL STUDIES
Past Perfume News

What to Do
Explain to students that incense and perfumes have been around since ancient civilizations. The ancient Egyptians were probably the most knowledgeable and obsessive about scents as any civilization, either before or after. Perfume was important during some periods because people seldom bathed. Queen Elizabeth had public places scented before she arrived.

What to Say
Pick a time and place in history and investigate their relationship to scent. How important was it to them? Was it only for rich people or royalty? Where did they get the ingredients? What other purposes did scents serve? Present your findings to the class as if you were a TV news reporter filing a story.

Why It's Important
Sensory details can be a powerful way to understand a period in history. Information gathering will help students better understand details of the past, such as how people managed without flushing toilets or regular bathing.

Literature Link
Lone Wolf

by Kathryn Lasky
(2010). New York: Scholastic.

This richly imagined fantasy begins when a bear finds an abandoned wolf cub and raises him as her own. The cub Faolan eventually sets out to find his own kind. His keen sense od smell helps him find his way and avoid danger throughout his journey.

Read aloud passages that showcase the author's skill for melding facts about wolves with fantasy. Ask: *How does the world the author has created help us better appreciate the mindful use of the senses?*

More Books to Share

Appelt, K. (2004). *Kissing Tennessee.* New York: Harcourt.

Sarguis, Mickey, ed. (2003). *What's That Smell? The Science Behind Adolescent Odors.* Cincinnati, OH: Terrific Science Press.

Silverstein, A. (2002). *Smelling and Tasting.* Brookfield, CT: Twenty-First Century Books.

HEALTH
Bacteria: the "B" in B.O.

What to Do
Explain to students that as they get older you may notice that your body begins to give off new and different smells. These are not always so pleasant. You may have to brush your teeth to keep your mouth fresh. You have to wash your body more often, especially after working up a sweat playing sports. What students may not realize is that they are not to blame for the bad smells—it is the bacteria that grows on them.

What to Say
It's the bacteria on and in your body that creates what we call "B.O." Now that you know that, let's research some tips for keeping the smelly bacteria at bay. Choose an odor problem to investigate. Then work with a partner to make a poster that explains how bacteria makes you smell and how to beat the bad bacteria.

Why It's Important
It our culture, it is important not to smell bad. However, it is also a very awkward subject to bring up. With students this age going through changes, they may not understand the odors they are giving off or what to do about them. This group activity allows students who need this information to get it in a way that is not personally stigmatizing.

SOCIAL-EMOTIONAL LEARNING
Perfume Power

What to Do
Explain to students that some people are more sensitive than others to scents. For example, young people, people with allergies, and those who have asthma may be more sensitive to strong scents. A condition called anosmia causes a person to lose the sense of smell completely. Smoking can damage your sense of smell, too.

What to Say
During the mindful smelling exercises you noticed that not everyone has the same feelings and associations with scents. In addition, not everyone is equally sensitive to smells. So what would you do if one person were wearing a heavy perfume that bothered someone else? Write a skit that shows how you'd handle this.

Why It's Important
Some students may need modeling to be able to speak up when they find a scent overpowering. Also, this exercise helps students become mindfully aware of differences and preferences among people.

Mindful Tasting

What Is Mindful Tasting?

To fully appreciate the food we eat—whether it's a complex treat, such as sweet grilled corn with hot chili and sour lime or a simple bowl of oatmeal—requires mindful tasting, or slowing down to savor our food and notice its flavor, texture, and temperature.

Why Practice Mindful Tasting?

Eating is something that is hardly ever done mindfully by young people. Mindful tasting can be a valuable task for demonstrating mindful awareness. A simple exercise of savoring and describing a morsel of food helps students understand the changes that can occur when an everyday act is performed slowly and with conscious attention to the experience.

Mindful tasting helps students identify discrete taste sensations, build descriptive skills, and approach food with a healthy outlook. It may also make them aware of the importance of healthful eating to their successful thinking and interacting at school. The exercise cues them to think carefully about what they're tasting and supports good digestion as they chew slowly and deliberately. With practice, students may be willing to try foods that are not part of their usual diet and make healthful food choices. Key social-emotional outcomes are building self-regulation skills and being accepting of new foods, which may lay the foundation for tolerance of cultural traditions outside of one's own.

What Can You Expect to Observe?

"Mindful tasting is a low-risk way for students to expand their attention and their palates. Students are more willing to taste something new when there are no expectations placed on their liking it or not. The non-judgmental atmosphere frees them to like or dislike whatever they try."

—Eighth-grade teacher

Linking to Brain Research

Relaxed and Alert:
The Role of Neurotransmitters

Neurotransmitters are key to the dynamic and ever-changing ecosystem of our brain. These chemical messengers influence a wide range of feelings and behaviors and are affected by sensory input and general health. Stress—real or perceived—causes changes in levels of neurotransmitters, including these three:

- Dopamine plays a crucial role in motivation, pleasure, and addiction and influences paying attention, planning, and moving the body.

- Serotonin contributes to the regulation of appetite, sleep, aggression, mood, and pain.

- Norepinephrine is important for attentiveness, emotions, sleeping, dreaming, and learning.

Increases and/or decreases in one or more of these neurotransmitter levels affect our mental state, and the feelings and behaviors generated by it. Attentiveness, engagement, competence, and achievement are only possible when a learner's brain is in a receptive state, allowing for calm and mindful response. Mindful tasting, like mindful seeing and smelling, gives children an opportunity to be both relaxed and aware. The novelty of this activity, along with children's curiosity and engagement help to balance neurotransmitters and produce a relaxed, yet very alert, state of mind. Mindful activities help train the prefrontal cortex to pay attention, absorb details, and think clearly.

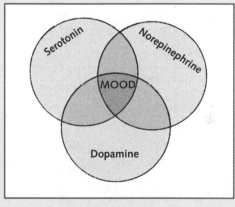

Levels and combinations of the neurotransmitters serotonin, norepinephrine, and dopamine influence our mental state.

Clarify for the Class

Use mindful tasting to compare sugar with artificial sweeteners. Give each student two small paper cups of a regular drink and a diet drink. Alternately, you could mix packets of sugar and artificial sweetener in water. Have students sample both, taking their time to savor each. Have them draw a Venn diagram to compare the tastes, textures, and smells of the sweetened drinks.

Discuss: Do you think you could tell the difference between the two in a blind taste test?

Getting Ready

You Might Like It
Capitalize on students' curiosity and broaden their cuisine options by challenging them to try a new food and describe it.

GOALS

- Students will focus their attention on savoring a morsel of food and describe their experience.
- Students will identify ways that mindful tasting can help them eat healthily.

MATERIALS

- food morsels that represent different flavor profiles (one per student), such as dates, raisins, watercress, radishes, pickle slices, dried cranberries, or anchovies.
- small napkins to place the food on

PREPARATION TIPS

- Be aware of any food allergies students may have and avoid high-risk foods such as nuts.
- Because this activity involves putting food in their mouths, have students wash their hands before the lesson.

CREATING THE OPTIMISTIC CLASSROOM

Supporting English Language Learners All students will benefit from vocabulary support, but ELLs will especially appreciate having a visual reference chart for the words. Bring in grocery circulars and have students cut out pictures of foods that fit each word (e.g., for salty, students might cut out potato chips and pretzels and for sour they might cut out lemons and pickles). Some words to include are: *sweet, spicy, salty, bland, crispy, sticky, chewy, crunchy, slimy, smooth, bitter, sour, juicy, dry, acidic, tender, tough, nutty, creamy, soft, hard, tart*

Mindful Food Choices
Encouraging students to mindfully taste healthy foods can help them appreciate fresh flavors and textures and choose better snacks.

MINDUP Warm-Up

Mindful Tasting Practice

Talk about the job of our taste buds and how they detect sweet, sour, bitter, and salty flavors. Ask students to choose one food to represent each of the four main flavors. Have them imagine one of the foods in front of them. For example, they might have picked a marshmallow, a green apple, a stalk of celery, and a potato chip.

Start by picturing this food in front of you. Now imagine the smell. Next, imagine bringing it to your lips. Let your mouth enjoy, or savor, the taste.

Have students repeat the exercise three more times for each of the different foods they picked.

Discuss: What did you notice in your body as you imagined each flavor? Could you taste it in your mouth? Did you notice any physical reactions, such as your mouth watering and lips puckering?

Leading the Lesson

A Matter of Taste

Engage

Explore

What to Do

Remind students of the four main flavors that were introduced during the warm-up activity. Then connect the idea of mindful tasting to other mindful sensing activities, listening, seeing, and smelling that students have experienced so far.

- Mindful tasting is a lot like mindful breathing. We all eat and breathe without thinking most of the time. That means most of the time we don't breathe deeply. And most of the time we don't really taste what we eat.

- The mindful tasting activity we'll do helps train our brains to focus on the flavors and textures of what we eat. Can you give some examples of the vocabulary we might use?

- When we practiced mindful smelling, our "specimens" were the canisters of scents. Today our "specimens" will be small pieces, or morsels, of food.

Remind students that their prefrontal cortex will be "on duty," working to notice every detail gathered by their RAS. Encourage the group to take a slow, deep breath to calm their amygdala and prepare to be mindful.

Give each student a morsel of food on a napkin. First have them mindfully look at their morsel, noticing the shape, the color, the size, and any markings on it.

Then have students close their eyes and focus on smelling the morsel. You may want to ask them if they'd like to share the associations the scent has for them. Ask volunteers to describe this scent as accurately as they can.

Finally, prompt students with cues that guide them to mindfully taste their morsel.

- Gently put the morsel in your mouth, but do not bite down yet! First, focus on how the morsel feels in your mouth. Is your mouth watering? Can you taste any flavors yet?

- Use your tongue to move the morsel around in your mouth. Think about how the texture of the morsel feels.

- Now, very slowly bite down and notice how easily it breaks apart. What flavors do you taste now? Chew it well and swallow slowly.

Why It's Important

In addition to providing students with another way to focus their minds, mindful tasting will help them appreciate the subtle flavors in food. This is important because when the subtle flavors can't be appreciated, people tend to rely on strongly sweet or salty flavors to excite their palates. These are usually not the healthiest food choices.

Be sure students notice how interconnected the senses of seeing, smelling, and tasting are. Just looking at the food may be enough to cause their mouths to water. Point out that smell is so important to taste that if their sense of smell were damaged, they would have a much harder time perceiving flavors. That is why food always tastes strange when we have colds.

Reflect

Invite students to compare and contrast how mindfully tasting a morsel is different from the way they typically eat food. Ask them how mindful tasting affects the flavor and the time it takes to eat.

- How long does it takes the brain to get the signal that the stomach is full? (10 to 15 minutes) Knowing that, how does mindful eating help you stop eating when you're full?

- If you eat quickly, why would you be more likely to grab strongly flavored foods, especially things that are very sweet or very salty? How does eating mindfully help you make healthier food choices?

Mindful tasting can have a positive impact on students' health and support better digestion. Eating mindfully encourages thorough chewing. By slowing down and paying attention, students can learn to recognize the signal that says they are full. Attention brought to flavors can help students appreciate subtle flavors from healthful, unprocessed foods.

MINDUP
In the Real World

Career Connection

Have professional taste buds, will report for work—that is, if you're a taste tester! Food scientists, who whip up all sorts of concoctions—from snack foods to beverages to condiments such as ketchup—conduct tests to comply with the standards and regulations that govern taste, texture, moisture, color, and nutrients as well as salt, fat, and sugar content. In order to meet quality controls, they rely on mindful tasters, who know how to use their tongues and taste buds to slowly, mindfully take in the full taste of every product. Taste testers might sample several dozen products and use a complicated scale to rate their choices.

Discuss: What might the differences and the similarities between the jobs of testers at a health food company and a candy company? How might their goals differ?

Once a Day

Instead of multitasking through lunch, take at least ten minutes to really taste (and digest) your food. You'll feel more satisfied, more able to focus, and more prepared to effectively manage the needs of your day.

Connecting to the Curriculum

Mindful tasting supports students' connection to their own learning process and to the content areas and literature.

Journal Writing

Encourage your students to reflect on what they've learned about mindful tasting and to record questions to explore at another time. They may also enjoy responding to these prompts:

- Make a menu for a meal that you would enjoy eating mindfully. Include any beverages and dessert. Describe the flavors and textures that would make this meal worth savoring.

- Write a poem that contains the four main flavors: sweet, bitter, sour, and salty. You can use the flavors to describe foods, or as metaphors to describe emotions, an experience you have had, or anything else you wish.

- Make a list of new foods to try. Some may be foods you have always wanted to try. Others may be foods that you have recently heard of. Whenever you try a new food, take notes. Do your best to describe the flavors and texture.

- Write a how-to manual for mindful tasting. What instructions would you give to someone you wanted to teach how to eat food mindfully? How would you explain the advantages?

the Optimistic classroom™ journal

SCIENCE
Supertasters

What to Do
Students may be interested to learn that things do not taste alike to all of us. Scientists have found that some people are supertasters. They actually have more taste buds and experience all flavors more intensely. They usually prefer bland foods, can't stand bitter or spicy flavors, and don't care for creamy or sweet foods. They tend to use a lot of salt to cover up any bitterness they taste.

What to Say
Does "supertaster" describe you or someone you know? Do a little more research on supertasters. Work with a group to design an experiment or survey that will help us discover who the supertasters are. We can review the ideas from each group and then decide as a class which ones to try.

Why It's Important
Practicing the scientific method with a real-world problem is a great way for students to apply that knowledge. In addition, teaching students about the variety of sensory experiences helps them develop more tolerance for individual differences. For example, a younger sibling who is extremely picky may be a supertaster. It also may give students greater insight into their own tastes.

LANGUAGE ARTS
Four Flavors Cookbook

What to Do
Have students contribute recipes for a class cookbook. Set up four groups, each focusing on one of the four main flavors: sweet, sour, bitter, and salty. Ask students to collect at least five recipes for their dominant flavor. In addition to the main flavor, have students tag their recipe with minor flavors and descriptions of texture. Teach students how to create an index.

What to Say
Together we will create a cookbook to satisfy a craving for any of the main flavors. Most recipes include more than one flavor, but you should be aware of the flavor that stands out. Your recipes should have clear instructions and a description of the finished dish. The description should describe how the dish should look, smell, and taste.

Why It's Important
This exercise will help students expand their palates. It is also an opportunity to explore a real-world writing genre.

SOCIAL STUDIES
Spice Story

What to Do

Bring in samples of pepper, cinnamon, cloves and nutmeg. Students may be surprised to learn that these spices made nations rich and changed the history of the world. They were used not just for seasoning, they were ingredients in perfume, they were used to preserve meat (before refrigerators), they were used for medicine, and they were even used to embalm the dead. Most of the spices that Europeans wanted came from Asia.

What to Say

Sample these spices and choose your favorite. Students who choose that spice will research its role in the spice trade. Find out which countries had it and which wanted it. Explain how that spice helped changed history. Include a map in your presentation, along with any other visual aids you wish.

Why It's Important

Bringing the spice to the fore of the lesson is an interesting way to explore the many important ramifications of the spice trade, including the European discovery of the Americas. After all, the discoveries were only a by-product of the hunt for spices, which was the focus of the explorers back then.

SOCIAL-EMOTIONAL LEARNING
Mindful Manners

What to Do

Students may be interested to learn that table manners and mindful eating have a lot in common. Both mindful eating and table manners include paying attention to your surroundings. Many people associate etiquette with formal dining, but there are many basic tips that work in any situation.

What to Say

Here are tips for having good table manners. See if you can make the connection to mindful eating. 1. Take a moment before you start. 2. Sit at the table with good posture. 3. Always try to taste some small amount of the food, even if it's not your favorite. 4. Do not talk with your mouth full. 5. Don't make loud or distracting noises when you eat, such as slurping or burping.

Why It's Important

This is a great opportunity to help students build important social skills they might not be aware of. As teens they will have exposure to new social situations and knowing some of the rules of polite eating (that are also mindful) will help make them more confident.

Literature Link
Granny Torrelli Makes Soup

by Sharon Creech
(2003). New York: Scholastic.

In this wise and funny book, Rosie helps her granny prepare soup and pasta. As Granny Torrelli cooks, she shares stories about her youth that bring to mind problems that Rosie and her friend Bailey are facing. Along the way, the wonderful food, mindfully prepared and shared help heal a rift between two best friends. Connect to discussions of comfort foods and how sharing a meal can enhance mindful tasting.

More Books to Share

Gay, K. (2009). *The Scoop on What to Eat.* Berkeley Heights, New Jersey: Enslow Publishers.

Horvath, P. (2001). *Everything on a Waffle.* New York: Garrar Strauss Giroux.

Winter, R. (2009). *A Consumer's Dictionary of Food Additives.* New York: Three Rivers Press.

the Optimistic classroom™ library

Mindful
Movement I

What is Mindful Movement?

How often are we conscious of putting weight on each part of the sole of our foot as we walk? Being alert to the sensations of the body, whether we are active or at rest, is a fundamental step in increasing mindful awareness.

Why Practice Mindful Movement?

Our body and brain are partners. We get burned and the nerve cells in our skin send a signal to our brain that registers pain. We get nervous and tense about an important test and our brain sends a signal to our body to sweat and cool down.

To move mindfully is to pay close attention to the sensations of our body when it is at rest and when it is active—the body gives us signals we can easily recognize to help us monitor physical and mental states such as exertion and stress.

In this lesson, students compare the signals their body sends after physical exertion and relaxation. They begin to learn simple self-regulation skills by controlling their breathing and heart rate. Developing an understanding of the brain-body relationship helps students become better able to identify the signals their body is sending and to manage their emotions and behaviors in response.

What Can You Expect to Observe?

"Students were skeptical at first, saying that being able to control your heart rate is something that only happens in science fiction stories. So you can imagine how excited they were that they were able to make it happen with controlled movement and breathing. They enjoy this practice and the power they feel they are gaining over their physiological responses."

—Sixth-grade teacher

Linking to Brain Research

Cortisol, the Stress Hormone

During a period of severe or persistent threat—perceived or real—the adrenal glands release extra cortisol, a hormone. Low levels of cortisol in the brain help us remain alert, and a sudden surge of the stress hormone is important in dealing with immediate danger. However, too much cortisol for too long can harm the brain and impair thinking, memory, and learning. High cortisol levels interfere with the function of neurotransmitters and can damage the hippocampus, which makes and stores memories. Excessive cortisol can make it hard to think and remember—"going blank" during a crisis may be an example of cortisol interference.

Brains in a constant state of alert due to physical, environmental, or emotional stress can have chronically elevated cortisol levels. During the crucial early years of brain development, high cortisol levels sustained over prolonged periods can cause significant damage and result in emotional dysfunction. Twenty-first century life brings many stressors to children at an early age: lack of downtime, parental stresses, pressures to achieve, exposure to violence, over-stimulating or noisy environments, families dealing with substance abuse, unrealistic expectations, and poverty. As children learn to mindfully regulate their own breathing and heart rate, they learn to lessen their stress level and enable a healthy emotional balance.

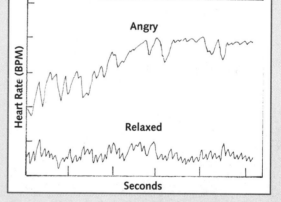

Our state of mind affects heart rate. The heart of someone who is angry can beat twice as fast as that of a relaxed person.

Clarify for the Class

Tell students they'll observe the connection between mind and body by measuring their heart rate before and after controlled breathing, which can slow our heart rate. Have them find their pulse after active small-group work, when heart rates may be slightly elevated. Then have them measure heart rates again immediately after doing the core practices. (Need to know how to take a pulse? See page 87, Warm-Up, and page 88, Explore.)

Discuss: Did the controlled breathing exercise alter heart rates? By how much, on average? What situations make your heart beat quickly? How could controlled breathing help you think clearly and make decisions during times of stress?

Getting Ready

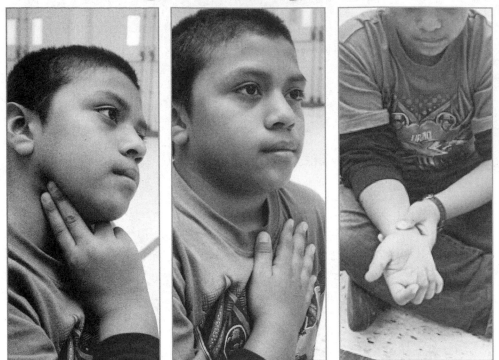

Pulse Awareness
Students learn to take a pulse in several ways.

GOALS
- Students will focus their attention on internal physical sensations, in both a relaxed and an active state.
- Students will monitor their own heart rate and exercise control over breathing and heart rate.

MATERIALS
- chart paper
- clock with second hand or stop watch

PREPARATION TIPS
- Make space in the classroom for students to do simple exercises safely around their desks, or find a clear area such as the gym or an outdoor court.
- For students with special physical needs, discuss appropriate adjustments for the active part of this lesson with the PE teacher, nurse, and parents, as needed.

CREATING THE OPTIMISTIC CLASSROOM
English Language Learners ELLs are especially prone to overactive amygdala functions and elevated cortisol levels. This is because it takes extra effort to communicate in a language in which you are not yet fluent, which often generates anxiety about missing important information. Between higher-intensity activities, help ELLs and all students rebuild positive neurotransmitters with a short "brain break," such as listening to music, having a discussion with classmates, or doing some free reading. This allows the brain to return to an optimal state for learning.

Exercise Calms You Down?
Students can take their resting
pulse before and after exercise to
determine whether exercise helped
them relax and feel better.

MINDUP Warm-Up

True and Pulse

Ask students to decide if the following heart facts are true or false: 1. The body's
blood vessels are 60,000 miles long—more than long enough to circle the globe
twice! 2. It only takes 20 seconds for blood to circulate through the entire vascular
system. 3. The heart beats about 100,000 times a day. Believe it or not, all those facts
are true!

Tell students that they are going to learn to do what good athletes do: find and
monitor their pulse without the need for any special equipment.

Demonstrate and have students practice finding their own heartbeat in any
of these ways:

- Hold one hand palm up; press the index and middle finger of the other hand on
  your wrist just below your palm;
- Press the index and middle finger of one hand at the top of your neck, just under
  your jaw (about midway between your earlobe and chin):
- Press your index and middle finger firmly at the center of the base of the throat.

Discuss: Which pulse point do you find easiest to use? When is it easier to find your
pulse, when you have just been active or when you are resting?

Leading the Lesson

Pulse Power

Engage

What to Do

Review finding a pulse point from the warm-up activity. Explain that an elevated, or stronger and faster, pulse shows the heart is working hard to supply oxygenated blood. The body does this when it is active because the muscles have a greater need for oxygen. The heart beats faster during times of emotional stress too. It's how the amygdala gets you ready for flight or fight. Just as we learned to control our breathing and clear our minds, we can also learn to bring down our heart rates.

- A normal pulse rate can be anywhere from 60 to 100 beats per minute. How fast do you predict your heart is beating right now?

- How could we change our pulse rates from slower to faster? How could we change from faster to slower?

Write down their ideas for slowing their pulse and elevating it. (Students will likely suggest some exercise, such as jumping jacks, to elevate their pulse and breathing exercises or the Core Practices to slow it down.)

Explore

Have students vote on the pulse-raising activity. Then have students engage in a few minutes of a pulse-elevating activity. Jumping jacks, running in place, even dancing would all work. Before students begin, have them take and record their resting pulse. Then have them take their pulse again after it's been elevated.

- First, find your pulse point and count the beats for 10 seconds. Your partner can keep time while you do this. Multiply this by six to get your beats per minute. Record your resting pulse.

- When I give the signal to start, you'll begin moving in order to elevate your pulse. When I give the signal to stop, stop and take your pulse again.

Here's where the science comes in. Divide the class into two groups. Have one group sit quietly. They can do free reading or some other seat work. Have the other group do a mindful breathing exercise. Have them sit comfortably with their eyes cast down or closed. Remind them to relax their muscles and focus on deep breathing. Ask the group of mindful breathers to open their eyes and look up at you when they feel their pulse slow down. Then have all the students retest their pulse rates.

Why It's Important

This can be an exciting scientific experiment for students who have been learning about the Core Practice. Until now, all the evidence that the Core Practice works has been subjective and anecdotal. This will be the first opportunity for students to see objective evidence of what mindful focusing can do and how much more in control of their bodies they can be.

Students enjoy discussing and comparing heart rates with peers and helping each other check their pulses. Generally, those who are fitter tend to have a lower resting pulse and quicker recovery rate. But students should not worry too much or feel competitive with others because pulse rates can vary a lot from day to day, even for the same person.

From the Research

Exercise ... optimizes your mind-set to improve alertness, attention, and motivation.
(Ratey, 2008)

Reflect

Invite students to discuss the way they created physical changes in their body through movement and mindful focus.

- You were able to drive your pulse to a fast rate and also slow it down. What other signals did you detect as you exercised more and your heart rate rose?

Students will likely answer that their skin got sweaty, their faces got flushed, and their whole body felt warmer. Guide students to understand that the brain signaled these changes to help the body cool down in order to perform better as it exercised. Review the changes they experienced as they slowed down.

- Which group had a lower pulse after five minutes, the group that sat quietly or the group that breathed mindfully?

- Are there other times when you're not exercising, but when your emotions may be taking charge, that your body might be sending similar signals? What can you do to help yourself?

Brainstorm reasons for any unexpected results. For example, recovery rate (the time it takes your pulse to return to normal) is a measure of physical fitness. As fitness improves, the recovery rate gets quicker. Explain that although exercise and anxiety both raise the pulse, exercise is also a good technique for reducing anxiety, because it leads to the release of dopamine, the natural feel-good chemical, in the brain.

MINDUP
In the Real World

Career Connection

A tai chi (Tie-CHEE) instructor teaches the ancient art of "meditation in motion," which connects mind and body and promotes serenity through gentle movements. Originally developed in ancient China for self-defense, tai chi has evolved into a noncompetitive, self-paced system of postures or movements performed in a slow, mindful manner. Each posture flows into the next without pause; there are more than 100 possible movements and positions, all of them coordinated with breathing.

Discuss: If you have a dream job, what types of movement does it require—fine eye-hand coordination (visual arts) or some kind of physical presentation? How would doing that movement mindfully help you do that job well?

Once a Day

Notice students' posture after they've been working in one place for a while—how well they hold themselves upright reflects their degree of alertness. Take short breaks to allow them to move (e.g., shaking out or doing a few jumping jacks), refresh, and refocus as needed.

Connecting to the Curriculum

Mindful movement supports students' connection to their own learning process and to the content areas and literature.

Journal Writing

Encourage your students to reflect on what they've learned about mindful movement and to record questions to explore at another time. They may also enjoy responding to these prompts:

- How many meanings are there for the word *heart*? Look it up in the dictionary. You'll find a number of meanings and expressions. Try to come up with an original sentence for each meaning. Can you use any of the expressions, too?

- Keep an exercise diary for a week. Write down how you feel before and after you do exercise of any kind. Summarize your results.

- Diagram the signals you get from your body when you raise your pulse through some kind of movement. Draw an outline of your body, with callouts to label the changes it goes through.

- Does a part of your body not feel quite right? Maybe you have an upset stomach, a banged toe, or even a bad haircut! Imagine this body part could talk. Write an imaginary dialogue you might have with it.

MATH
Heart Rate Data Analysis

What to Do

Everyone's heart rate is unique, and collecting that data is a good opportunity to practice some statistical analysis. Students should know that that the mean, or average, is the total divided by the number of participants. They can find the median by lining up the data in order and counting to the midpoint. If there is an even number in the set, the two midpoints are averaged. The mode is the most frequent pulse rate.

What to Say

Have students use the data that they collected during the lesson's main activity and apply the mean, median, and mode to do a statistical analysis. If that data has already been lost, students can replicate the main activity as it is or simplify it by simply recording their resting pulses. Encourage students to chart the results on a line graph.

Why It's Important

This activity gives students a practical application for math. Capitalize on their fascination with gathering data from their own efforts and comparing their data with that of their peers. In addition to finding the mean, median, and mode, the presentation of the data in graph form is another useful application of important math skills.

SCIENCE
Look Into Your Heart

What to Do

Have students do some research on the amazing human heart. You may wish to have students find their own resources online or in the library.

What to Say

Work with a partner to do some research on the human heart, taking notes when you find something interesting. It is such an amazing organ that you should have no trouble making a top-ten list of fascinating heart facts. Make your list in the style of a countdown, saving the most interesting fact of all for last. Create visual aids to go with your presentation, if you wish.

Why It's Important

Learning how the heart works is a great way to motivate students to care for their heart health. Point out that smoking is linked to heart disease. Other mood-altering substances can damage the heart by causing it to beat too quickly or to stop beating altogether. Students can use this information to make better choices about their health.

LANGUAGE ARTS
A Poem from the Heart

What to Do
Choose a few examples of poems with pronounced rhythms. You could choose any sonnet by Shakespeare or Edgar Allan Poe's "The Raven." Explain that poems written in meter have a pattern of stressed (/) and unstressed syllables (x). Some common patterns are iambic (x/) or troachic (/x). Other patterns include anapestic (xx/) or dactylic (/xx). Point out how everyone's heartbeat is also in a pattern of stressed and unstressed beats.

What to Say
You will need someone to listen to your heartbeat. A tube from a roll of paper towels works very well for this purpose. Have them say the beat out loud using nonsense words, like ba-DUM-bum. Write down what you hear. Turn that rhythm into a poetic meter. See if you can change the nonsense words into a poem.

Why It's Important
Some students find poetry very abstract. This activity lets them connect physically with their own internal music and be inspired by it. It is also a fun introduction to classic works that are written in meter.

If students are not comfortable having a classmate close enough to listen to their heartbeat, allow them to gather this data at home.

SOCIAL-EMOTIONAL LEARNING
Couch Potato Blues

What to Do
Brainstorm with students activities that can counteract their sedentary habits, and assess the relative merits of inactive and active choices. Being active helps maintain a healthy weight, reduces blood pressure, raises good cholesterol, reduces the risk of diabetes and some kinds of cancer, and improves coordination and emotional well-being.

What to Say
Since being active keeps our hearts and brains healthy, let's brainstorm some ordinary after-school activities. Let's put our ideas onto a T-chart, dividing them into "active" and "inactive." Then we can rate them on a scale from zero to ten. Zero is not moving at all; ten is working very hard.

Why It's Important
Childhood obesity and lack of fitness are serious public health problems. Young people are leading a more sedentary existence than any previous generation. Teaching students the importance of physical activity can help them address the problem.

Literature Link
Everest, Book 1 (The Contest)

by Gordon Korman
(2002). New York: Scholastic.

Talk about your ultimate physical challenge. But that's not all. It's a mental challenge as well. Find out who will be the youngest person to climb Mount Everest. Is winning the contest worth everything—even if lives are at stake?

Connect this exciting adventure story to the mind/body connection students learned about in this lesson. Discuss how people can prepare for extreme physical tests by training their bodies with exercise and training their minds with focus.

More Books to Share

Corbin, Charles, Guy Le Masurier, and Dolly Lambdin. (2007). *Fitness for Life Middle School*. Champaign, IL: Human Kinetics.

Giovanni, Nikki. (2008). *Hip Hop Speaks to Children: A Celebration of Poetry with a Beat*. Naperville, IL: Sourcebooks Jabberwocky.

Nixon, Shelley. (1999). *From Where I Sit: Making My Way with Cerebral Palsy*. New York: Scholastic.

Mindful
Movement II

What More Can We Learn About Mindful Movement?

Mindful movement begins with the awareness of our constantly changing physical sensations, as described in Lesson 8. We can build on this awareness by using movement challenges to help our brains focus and work more efficiently.

Why Revisit Mindful Movement?

In this second lesson on mindful movement, students continue to deepen their awareness of physical sensations they often overlook. From their Pulse Power activity in the last lesson, students learned how to exercise vigorously to accelerate their heart rate and use breathing to calm their heart; they discovered that they could both mindfully observe and help control their physical responses. With this understanding, students are ready to try a set of physical challenges that require focus and concentration in order to maintain their balance. Participating in the balancing activity helps students deepen their brain-body connection and build self-regulation skills as they work to control their physical and emotional responses to stay steady.

In addition, students work on strengthening their decision-making abilities in this lesson. Working on our physical balance is shown to have positive effects on our brain's health, reinforcing higher-order thinking skills and emotional control.

What Can You Expect to Observe?

"Students enjoy balancing exercises because they're like a game. Also, since the results are visible, students can chart their own improvement, literally by the second. That is a big motivator. They take pride in their own accomplishments and encourage their classmates too."

—Seventh-grade teacher

Linking to Brain Research

Emotional Balance:
Key to Efficient Executive Function

Executive function is mental management that takes the big picture into account. Executive function comprises many higher-order skills that depend upon the thinker's ability to reflect before reacting. Among these skills are evaluating information, organizing, focusing attention, prioritizing, planning, and problem solving. The control of executive functions is guided by our prefrontal cortex, proportionally the largest of any primate. Executive function skills are affected by our emotional state in part because the neural networks for emotional response overlap with the neural networks for executive functions. Thanks to the brain's neuroplasticity, both of these overlapping networks in the prefrontal cortex are strengthened when the brain is engaged in either an emotional response or an executive function.

Learners who can recognize and control their own emotional state become confident and successful, both socially and academically. Neuroscientist Adele Diamond notes that "activities that often get squeezed out of school curricula, such as the arts and physical exercise, are excellent for developing executive function skills, improving children's emotional state and social skills, and can be critical for academic success and for success later in life" (2009). Engaging in physical challenges, the arts, and mindful practices that enhance learning and reduce stress activate both emotional response and executive function networks simultaneously.

Human Performance Chart

Performance

Optimum

Boredom

Burnout

Demands

Some stress is necessary to normal functioning, but ever increasing amounts of stress produce diminishing returns on learning, achieving, socializing, and living.

Clarify for the Class

Mindful walking combines mindfulness with movement. Model how to walk with good posture, and count your breaths coming in through your nose and going out through the mouth. Count out loud so that students can see how you match the counts for inhalation and exhalation. Do a talk-aloud as you notice each step, how each foot comes down, what your arms are doing, and how your posture is. Demonstrate how to bring stray thoughts back to your breathing and moving body.

Discuss: What effect do you think mindful walking has on the emotions? Explain. Why do you think physical movement can help us process information? Does it help you?

Getting Ready

Straight and Tall
Bring balance practice that begins in the gym back to the classroom. Balance breaks taken beside a desk can improve focus and posture.

GOALS
- Students mindfully control their balance and describe the sensations they experience.
- Students will connect mindful balancing to being well balanced in life.

MATERIALS
- four of each: plastic spoons, cups of water, empty cups

PREPARATION TIPS
- Make space in the classroom for students to do simple exercises safely around their desks, or find a clear area such as the gym or an outdoor court.
- Students will need comfortable, non-slip shoes, such as sneakers, for this activity. If done in bare feet, non-slip mats might be helpful.
- For those with special physical needs, seek advice from the PE teacher, nurse, and/or parents.

CREATING THE OPTIMISTIC CLASSROOM
Classroom Management Here are some ideas for creating a relaxed, brain-friendly classroom environment:
- limit periods of sitting and listening
- plan time for peer-talk to cement learning
- when possible allow students choice of activities and materials
- when appropriate and not at the expense of anyone else, encourage laughter
- offer immediate positive feedback when possible

Challenge Me!
Students with well-developed balancing skills can try more difficult moves on a thick mat while keeping a beanbag steady on their head.

MINDUP Warm-Up

Steady as You Go

Divide the class into four teams. Each team gets a spoon, a cup of water, and an empty cup. The object is to fill the spoon with water, walk it from one point in the room to another, and dump the water in the empty cup.

Explain that this activity is a bit like a relay race, but speed is not important. Mindful balance is. Introduce the terms *balance*, *steady*, and *stable*. Tell students that each member of the team will get a chance to walk with the spoonful from the beginning point to the end point. If each team does not have an even number of students, choose a student who will go twice.

Discuss: Which group has transferred the most water into the empty cup? What was your best strategy for holding the spoon steady? How did you keep it stable in your hand? What did you learn about mindful balance from this activity?

Leading the Lesson

Stable and Able

Engage

What to Do

Review how students have learned to observe the sensation signals their body sends and how to use their breath and mindful focus to calm down when needed. Relate the mindful walking in the warm-up to the next movement experience.

- Think about everything you've learned from your Core Practices and mindful control over your movement and senses.

- To get us started, think about how you carried a spoonful of water for you team. What helped you feel balanced and steady? When did you feel shaky and unstable?

Encourage students to share times when they've felt both balanced and unbalanced. Make sure they can connect focusing and paying close attention to being able to be balanced and steady.

Why It's Important

Learning how to apply what they've learned to physical balance has several healthy benefits. It teaches good posture, without which it would be very difficult to balance. It strengthens core muscles. But most importantly, good balance helps to prevent accidents.

Explore

Guide students through the first balancing exercise. Encourage them to stand in an open space and focus by taking a few deep breaths and feeling their feet on the ground. Then have them stand on tiptoes for 60 seconds.

- Remember to breathe deeply and pay close attention to the sensations in your feet and legs. You can touch your heels down, if your leg muscles get too tired or feel unsteady.

- If you are having trouble balancing, focus your eyes on one spot. Don't look over at anyone else.

- Does it help you balance if your mind is quiet?

For the second exercise, have students balance on one leg for 60 seconds. Repeat coaching.

Starting with an easier challenge builds students' confidence. Allow students who are feeling very challenged to repeat the first activity, until they feel comfortable trying the next one; tell them that when they find a less wobbly position they can add to the challenge by closing their eyes. Encourage students with experience in yoga, dance, gymnastics, martial arts, or skateboarding to share tips with peers.

Reflect

Invite students to discuss the increased challenge of the second activity and what they did to help themselves stay steady.

- Did this activity get difficult for you at any point? Did focusing your eyes on a single point help you balance? Was anyone able to close their eyes?

- What did your brain say to you during this activity? Did it help to focus your mind on breathing to quiet it down?

- When could you practice mindful balancing? Why might that help you?

Make sure the class covers these key points:
- When our bodies and brains work together, we can focus and think clearly.

- When we pay attention to the signals our body sends, our brain's ability to focus improves.

- Like all the other mindful activities, mindful movement and balancing helps our prefrontal cortex practice focusing.

As students master easy balance challenges, they may want to push their brain and body further. Encourage students to extend the time they spend in each balancing position. Teach advanced students a new balancing pose or have them invent some of their own. Check back with students and allow them to teach new poses to their classmates.

MINDUP
In the Real World

Career Connection

Imagine walking on a narrow beam of steel more than 1,000 feet in the air. If you're a high-rise ironworker, mindful movement—combining graceful agility with a keen sense of balance—not only enables you to do your job, but also helps guarantee your survival. When you're 100 flights up, overlooking a busy city street, one false step could mean a tumble to your death. While ironworkers take safety precautions such as ropes, harnesses, and safety nets, their best hope for survival is their own mindful movement—while being completely tuned in to all that's going on around them.

Discuss: Mindful movement on the job may mean the slow, graceful movement of a painter or mindful movement to avoid danger. How do you see both at play in the movements of Olympic athletes?

Once a Day

Try a simple balancing action such as standing on one foot, whenever you or your students are waiting (e.g., in line at the cafeteria, prior to dismissal). Balancing takes no preparation and keeps students focused and aware.

Connecting to the Curriculum

Expanding their experience of mindful movement supports students' connection to their own learning process and to the content areas and literature.

Journal Writing

Encourage your students to reflect on what they've learned about mindful movement and to record questions to explore at another time. They may also enjoy responding to these prompts:

- Think of something in your life that needs more balance. Brainstorm a list of ideas for improving the situation. Use these questions to get yourself started: Can you adjust the time, energy, or brain space you spend?

- Choose a role model for balance. Write a letter to this person. Let them know why they exemplify balance for you. It can be their physical balance you admire or the ability to balance different activities.

- When you get homework in more than one subject, you must learn to balance your effort. Rate yourself on a scale from one to ten. One means there's lots of room for improvement. Ten means that you have perfect balance. Explain your rating and how you can improve it.

- Give yourself a week-long balancing challenge. Take a few minutes to practice a mindful balancing activity. Each day write down the pose you held and how long you held it. At the end of the week, describe any improvements you noticed.

the Optimistic™ classroom journal

SCIENCE
Zero-G Balance

What to Do
Invite students to research how astronauts prepare for zero gravity. They will find that the inner ear and visual orientation are responsible for balance here on earth. However, in space there is no gravity and no up or down. People in zero gravity often get motion sickness. Astronauts must learn how to adapt so they can get their work done. Check the BBC's "Vomit Comet" video if appropriate (http://www.bbc.co.uk/learningzone/clips/balance-in-zero-gravity/1867.html).

What to Say
If you think mindful balancing exercises are difficult, try floating around in space without any gravity! Here on earth, your sense of balance depends on the downward pull of gravity on your body's mass. So how do astronauts train to find their balance in a zero G environment? Do some research and report back to the class.

Why It's Important
Finding balance in a zero-G environment highlights the interplay of factors that help us find and maintain our balance. This is also a good opportunity to tie balance to the concept of mass and gravity, which helps make it less abstract.

ARTS
Dance It On

What to Do
Dance is an art that embodies balance. Have students make up their own dance moves using the balancing skills they learned. Begin by taking some recommendations from students for a song. (Remind students that the song choices need to be appropriate for a school setting.) Once there are a few acceptable choices, let students vote.

What to Say
Think about your best dance move. Raise you hand if you would like to share it with the class. I'll take down names in alphabetical order. Form a circle, and when the music starts, I'll call the first name. That person will go in the center of the circle and show off their move. Everyone in the circle will try to copy it.

Why It's Important
This activity gives students a chance to practice balance. It also allows volunteers a chance to lead the group, while those not comfortable leading still get to participate. Students who may not normally take a leadership role have a chance to shine.

WALTER DEAN MYERS

AWARD-WINNING AUTHOR OF *SOMEWHERE IN THE DARKNESS* AND *MONSTER*

SLAM!

SOCIAL STUDIES
A Balance of Powers

What to Do

One of the great things about our government is the way the Founding Fathers designed the balance of powers. In fact, James Madison said, "The accumulation of all powers, legislative, executive, and judiciary, in the same hands, whether of one, a few, or many, and whether hereditary, self-appointed, or elected, may justly be pronounced the very definition of tyranny." Provide some reference materials that students can use.

What to Say

Work with a group to demonstrate the balance of power among the three branches of government. You can be as creative as you like in your presentation. You can make visuals or act out a skit. You could even write a rap. Anything you decide is fine as long as you explain how the powers of government are divided up. Try to incorporate into your explanation something you learned about balancing your body.

Why It's Important

Connecting an abstract idea, such as the balance of powers in government, to a concrete lesson on balance is great way to build a brain connection. The balance of powers is a foundational social studies concept and this is an entertaining and unique way for students to reinforce their knowledge of it.

SOCIAL-EMOTIONAL LEARNING
It Takes Two

What to Do

Have partners try a balancing exercise for partners. They might face each other, join hands, lean back in opposite directions, and turn in a circle like that. Or partners can lean into each other back-to-back, then lower down into a squat, holding a book between their backs. Have students invent their own variations.

What to Say

How was it different to balance with a partner than on your own? Was it more difficult or easier? How well did you communicate? How much did you need to trust the other person? What did the exercise teach you about teamwork?

Why It's Important

This activity is a great way to teach teamwork. In a two-person balancing exercise, the effort must be equally shared in order to achieve balance. Neither person can take over or shirk. One person cannot shirk. Be sure students extract the metaphor and apply the lessons to the idea of teamwork during the discussion.

Literature Link
Slam!

by Walter Dean Myers
(1996). New York: Scholastic.

This is a story of Greg "Slam" Harris who has plenty of balance on the basketball court but is struggling to find his balance off it. A high school basketball star, Harris transfers to a more academically challenging school. He has to learn to be a team player, but that's not all. The problems in his family are even harder to balance.

Connect this book to what students have learned about balance on their own and when balance depends on teamwork.

More Books to Share

Hine, Lewis. (1997). *Men at Work*. Mineola, NY: Dover Publications.

Koontz, Robin. (2008). *Tai Chi for Fun*. Mankato, MN: Compass Point Books.

Ramthum, Bonnie. (2008). *White Gates*. New York: Random House.

the Optimistic classroom™ library

It's All About
Attitude

As students learn new ways to cultivate a positive mind-set, they prime their brain for learning and for building healthy relationships.

By looking at an event from different perspectives, students learn to mindfully consider viewpoints other than their own.

Students explore the meaning of optimism and pessimism and discover how these two attitudes affect our relationships and ability to learn.

This lesson demonstrates how recalling happy memories can help students regulate their emotions and maintain an optimistic attitude.

The findings of researchers in the field of psychology seem logical: cultivating happiness in our lives has myriad benefits emotionally, socially, and physically—we relate to others better, we treat ourselves well, and we are more likely to adopt healthy habits and avoid destructive behaviors.

But can happiness really help us get smarter? Yes! Cognitive studies have shown that learning that is connected with a happy or positive emotional experience causes the information to get stored in our long-term memories, while learning that takes place in conditions that cause stress and anxiety is stored only in short-term memory; it is not available for long-term use (Pawlak, et. al., 2003; Shadmehr & Holocomb, 1997).

That's a research-based incentive to bring more laughter and joy into our lessons. Helping students develop skills in relating better to others and making happy memories of what they learn are key goals of the three lessons in this unit.

Perspective Taking

What is Perspective Taking?

We live in a "small world" with as many different ways of seeing things as there are people. Perspective taking allows us to consider more than one way of understanding a behavior, event, or situation. This skill is particularly useful on a global scale as our ability to communicate and our need to share resources with other people and cultures expand.

Why Practice Perspective Taking?

On the most practical level, students who are able to accept that other classmates may behave or think differently than they do are much better equipped to tolerate and find ways to get along with peers. These students can talk out a problem and find a solution that is mutually agreeable.

Perspective taking, like the Core Practice and other mindful skills, simply takes practice to develop. As students routinely identify other perspectives, they learn to think with an "open mind"—to pause and consider other viewpoints mindfully.

This increasing ability to consider a situation in multiple ways has social benefits, such as reducing conflicts among students, facilitating group work, and cultivating an inclusive peer community. Perspective taking is an essential skill for problem solving in all subject areas, from understanding conflict in literature to finding alternative strategies for solving problems in math and science.

What Can You Expect to Observe?

"At first, I used the expression 'Let's flip it.' to cue students to think about different points of view. Now students are doing this spontaneously. They are very interested in how the same situation might affect people differently. This is making our class discussions more subtle and deeper."

—Seventh-grade teacher

Linking to Brain Research

Opening the Mind to the Prefrontal Cortex

Perspective taking is the ability to see situations and events from the viewpoint of another person. When we mindfully practice perspective taking, we become more skilled at accurately interpreting the behavior of those around us. Mentally standing in someone else's shoes requires reflection, which can forestall an unthinking reaction. Repeatedly viewing issues or events through different lenses builds and strengthens the neural networks that enable us to reason before we take action. Paying attention to a situation in a calm, focused, mindful manner is a physiological workout for the brain, actually stimulating blood flow to it. Calm perspective taking directs incoming information on to the reflective, thinking prefrontal cortex instead of to the reflexive, reacting amygdala.

As students learn to consider alternate points of view, they can more effectively quell their own anxieties, exercise impulse control, and gauge their own behaviors and reactions in response to others. When differences of opinion are honored, and disagreement is respectful, students perceive the classroom as safe and risk-free. This unstressed state of mind allows their amygdala to "stand down" and puts the prefrontal cortex in control. A brain that operates primarily in the prefrontal cortex makes superior decisions, facilitating good choices for its owner.

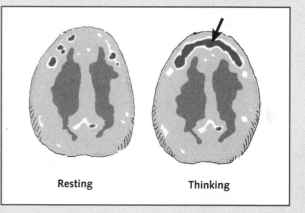

Resting   Thinking

These scans show where blood is flowing in the brain. Notice the increased blood flow in the prefrontal cortex area (arrow) of the thinking brain.

Clarify for the Class

Practicing origami is a good analogy for the building of neural pathways through repeated practices, such as perspective taking. Explain that refolding an already creased origami sheet goes faster, like the improved speed of a much-used chain of connected neurons. Help students fold a star, frog, or other simple origami figure. Next have them unfold the figure until it's a flat sheet again, then refold it into an origami figure.

Discuss: Why was it easier to fold the origami figure the second time? Was it faster, too? How is this like building and strengthening neural pathways? What repeated thoughts might help your brain to carefully consider actions before doing them?

Getting Ready

Character Contrasts
Students try to identify each
character's perspective in a fable.

GOALS
- Students identify different perspectives of characters in a story.
- Students apply open-minded perspective taking to social situations in their own lives.

MATERIALS
- book of African folktales, Greek myths, or Aesop's fables (Possible stories: Anansi the Spider, Demeter and Persephone, The Fox and the Grapes)
- Character Perspectives activity sheet (p. 156)

CREATING THE OPTIMISTIC CLASSROOM
Supporting English Language Learners Modeling the emotional component of written dialogue is especially helpful for second-language learners. It helps them build expressive language skills of stress placement and gesture to convey emotion. Have English-speaking volunteers read any dialogue from the story, using appropriate facial expressions and body language ("Those grapes are probably sour anyway!" said the wolf.) Understanding the emotional content of characters' words will help second-language learners understand and discuss different points of view.

More Brains, Better Ideas
Work on perspective-taking helps build group-work skills, such as a willingness to consider alternative ideas.

MINDUP Warm-Up

Perspective-Taking Practice

Explain that there is a famous parable of the six blind men and the elephant. None of them sees the whole elephant, but each touches a different part and forms a conclusion.

- The first man touches the trunk.
- The second man touches the leg.
- The third man touches the ear.
- The fourth touches the side.
- The fifth touches the tail.
- The sixth touches the tusk.

Introduce the term *perspective* and the term *conflict*, before you discuss what each man's experience of the elephant might have been.

Discuss: Have students form six groups and describe the elephant based on only one of its parts. Ask each group to prepare a statement they could use in a debate about what the elephant is like. Then as a class, talk about how the conflict might be resolved. Finally ask, "What might the elephant be used to represent?" (any situation or problem, or even reality itself).

Leading the Lesson

Get Into Their Heads

Engage

What to Do

Choose a traditional story, myth, or fable (see Materials for suggestions) to read aloud with the class. Select a story with a limited number of characters. Help students connect inferences they make about each character to the different perspectives in the warm-up activity.

- How can a character's actions and words help a reader figure out the character's point of view? (Their words and thoughts help you know what they want and don't want.)

- What other kinds of information can help you determine the character's perspective? (Descriptions and backgrounds can also tell you about a character.)

Have the class choose one character to study, display the Character Perspectives activity sheet, and lead students through a character-perspective analysis. Scribe answers from volunteers so that everyone has a record.

Explore

Invite students to rewrite the story from one character's point of view. Hand out copies of the activity sheet to pairs or groups of three.

- How does the perspective of this character change the story?

- Which characters might share a similar perspective?

- How does this character's perspective differ from the neutral perspective of a narrator?

Explore any conflicts this character has in the story. Discuss ways that these conflicts might be settled through a mutually beneficial agreement or a compromise.

Why It's Important

Story characters provide a good way to engage students in the study of perspective—and because the characters are fictional, students do not have a personal stake in the characters' conflicts. Encourage students to mindfully explore each character's perspective and motivation. If students begin to make judgments, remind them to keep a mindful and tolerant attitude.

Now that they're familiar with analyzing one character's perspective on a given event, they can use this perspective as a point of contrast to examine another character's perspective. Although the activity can be done independently, students benefit from group discussion in which they can clarify any confusion and narrow down their best ideas.

Reflect

Have students think about the story and how many
different ways it could have been told. Connect this
way of stepping back from the situation to see all the
different perspectives with other mindful exercises
they have done.

- When you try to understand something from
  someone else's point of view, you are "taking a
  different perspective." How is that like or unlike
  the mindful sensing activities we've been practicing?

Make sure students can connect that when they
sensed mindfully, they had to pay attention to what
their bodies were telling them. Now they are learning
to pay attention to their own thoughts and feelings
as well as those of other people in an interested,
nonjudgmental way.

- What happens to thinking once a judgment has
  been made?

- Are judgments ever appropriate? If so, when is
  the best time to make them?

- What would make you want to rethink your
  judgments?

This reflection should guide students to conclude that:
- Different people may have different reactions or
  opinions regarding the same fact or event

- Taking the time to mindfully consider others'
  perspectives helps us take in the larger situation
  and helps us form better judgments.

MINDUP
In the Real World

Career Connection

The writer I.A.R. Wylie once wrote,
*True generosity...requires imagination—
the capacity to see people in all their
perplexities and needs, and to know
how to expend ourselves effectively for
them.* Peace negotiators typically possess
both an abundance of imagination and
unique powers of persuasion. These
enable them to help those locked in
conflict to transcend their own views, take
the perspective of the other, and bend
toward a mutually acceptable solution.
"Walk a mile in my shoes" is another way
of saying "step outside of yourself and
imagine what it feels like to be me."

Discuss: How does sensitivity to multiple
perspectives matter in the work done by
social workers, teachers, and writers?

Once a Day

Each day, choose one student to focus on.
Observe the student closely; listen in on
class conversations; talk one-on-one. Your
attention can help you better understand
how that student approaches work and
relationships—invaluable for building
community and differentiating instruction.

Connecting to the Curriculum

Perspective taking supports students' connection to their own learning process and to the content areas and literature.

Journal Writing

Encourage your students to reflect on what they've learned about perspective taking and to record questions to explore at another time. They may also enjoy responding to these prompts:

- Rethink your last disagreement with someone. Take the part of the other person. Write yourself a letter from the other person's perspective. What did you learn by thinking about the issue from the opposite side?

- What makes your perspective unique? Write a recipe for it. First think about a list of possible ingredients, such as values, desires, needs, experiences. Then think about the proportions. Be creative!

- Take an issue and break it down on a Venn diagram, for example, school uniforms: yes or no? Which points are disputed? Which points could the two sides agree on? Use the diagram to suggest a possible solution or compromise.

- Think of a villain from a book, movie, TV show, or even a video game. Tell the story from this perspective. Is there any way to make this character slightly more sympathetic by shifting the perspective?

the Optimistic classroom™ journal

LANGUAGE ARTS
Plot Drivers

What to Do
Explain that all plots are driven by a problem or conflict. Often, the conflict starts from a misunderstanding. Choose a story that is based on a misunderstanding, for example Jane Austen's *Pride and Prejudice*. Students can watch it on DVD or read an accessible version (see the Read 180 library), or read it in graphic novel form. There is even a version with zombies! Preview the plot with students beforehand.

What to Say
Choose one of the main characters to analyze. Think about: What perspective is this character missing? Which other character or characters have this perspective? What is preventing this character from gaining a bigger perspective? Does the character finally achieve a more complete understanding? How does the character get this knowledge? How would the story change if this character had this understanding sooner?

Why It's Important
Identifying plot conflicts and engaging in character analysis are important skills in language arts. Understanding how three-dimensional characters handle conflicts is also a good way for students to understand the relationships in their own lives.

SOCIAL STUDIES
Deadly Conflicts

What to Do
Have students select a historical war that interests them. Assign two students to research each war. Each student will represent one of the warring parties. Then have students working on the same war summarize their respective viewpoints to the class without stating which side they represent. See if the class can figure that out from the perspective of each summary.

What to Say
Wars happen when groups are unable to resolve their conflicts. Explore the different sides in one actual war. Summarize the conflict from the perspective of one side. Push your point of view as strongly as possible—make no attempt to be fair and evenhanded! Your classmates will try to guess the conflict and which side you represent.

Why It's Important
By concentrating on the issues of one side at a time and hearing a classmate present the other side, students will gain a deeper understanding of the most destructive conflict of all—war.

ART/MATH
Picture Perspective

What to Do
Show students a drawing of a three-dimensional shape, such as a cube, and have them identify it. Explain that during the Renaissance in Europe, artists developed a theory of perspective, applying principles of geometry to drawing to make objects appear to occupy space in a realistic way. Perspective gives the illusion of depth, representing a third dimension.

What to Say
Before people knew how to use perspective, the figures they drew were two-dimensional, or flat. Try it. Draw a horizon line. Draw a tree in the foreground, then draw a line to a point on the horizon from the top and bottom of that tree where the lines meet. The vanishing point is the vertex. Draw more trees inside that angle so they get smaller in the distance. Compare your drawings. Do any two have the identical perspective?

Why It's Important
Understanding perspective completely changed the way artists depict reality. Students can play with this activity to see how relocating the horizon line and vanishing point, changes the perspective. This will concretize an important art-historic milestone, as well as a fundamental math concept.

SOCIAL-EMOTIONAL LEARNING
Conflict Resolution

What to Do
Have students construct a conflict resolution rubric they can use to settle minor disputes among themselves. Consider these steps: attitude, listening, explaining, brainstorming, agreement, follow-up. Have students describe how each step could be done mindfully. Then have students role-play a conflict while their classmates use the rubric to grade them.

What to Say
Let's work in groups. Each group will describe how one step of the process could be done mindfully. Once we have created the rubric, two volunteers can choose a situation of conflict to resolve by role-play, while the rest of you use the rubric to grade them.

Why It's Important
Conflict resolution depends on listening to another person's perspective and being relaxed enough to engage the PFC in mutual problem solving. With practice, students will be able to use conflict resolution skills to defuse conflicts before they escalate.

Literature Link
Nothing But the Truth

by Avi
(1991). New York: Scholastic.

Ninth grader Philip Malloy is only trying to get his English class transferred but the "facts" of his story get twisted and snowball into a major national scandal. Many characters give their point of view, and the story is told in a variety of genres: journal entries, letters, memos, and dialogues.

Students will be able to connect this story to the idea of multiple perspectives and how the truth can be distorted by rushing to judgment and a failure to communicate.

More Books to Share

Avi, and Rachel Vail. (2005). *Never Mind! A Twin Novel*. New York: HarperCollins.

Vande Velde, Vivian. (2001). *The Rumpelstiltskin Problem*. New York: Scholastic.

VanDraanen, Wendelin. (2003). *Flipped*. New York: Knopf.

the Optimistic™ classroom library

Choosing
Optimism

What Is Optimism?

Optimism is a way of seeing life hopefully and having an expectation of success and well-being. Optimism correlates strongly with good health and effective coping strategies. Optimism is a learned trait and, if practiced, can become a way of thinking.

Why Practice Optimism?

Choosing to view life optimistically can increase our brain capacity; it relaxes our amygdala, creates chemical balance in our brains, and allows our prefrontal cortex to take charge. In this frame of mind, students learn that they can make much better choices than if they take a negative or pessimistic approach, which effectively shuts down their higher-level thinking.

Practicing optimism also makes it easier to learn—optimistic thinkers prime their brains to be ready to focus and make more room for new information to be absorbed and new ideas to stretch their wings. Socially, practicing optimism allows students to strengthen their perspective-taking skills and accept viewpoints different from their own, as well as connect with other people. In this lesson, students explore the benefits of optimism and see how the "dark cloud" of pessimism negatively affects their ability to think and learn, make friends, and solve common problems. With a pessimistic attitude, a person can get bogged down and limit his or her ability to solve problems.

What Can You Expect to Observe?

"Feeling tossed in a tempest of emotion is a way of life for middle school students. They, more than anyone, need a rudder-like tool that allows them to change direction. It makes the difference between feeling like a victim of your emotions or that you have some control."

—Eighth-grade teacher

Linking to Brain Research

Optimism: A Learned Skill for Success

The research is clear—attitude matters! Students who are generally optimistic enjoy better physical health, have more success at school, flourish in relationships, and are more well equipped to handle stress in their lives. Brain research has confirmed that optimism is more a learned trait than a genetic one. We can train our brain to have an optimistic perspective, thanks to neuroplasticity. This brain process forms new branching-off dendrites and more neuron-to-neuron connections during repeated experiences and practice. When students regularly use self-talk for positive thinking and to work through everyday frustrations, neuroplasticity creates and strengthens nerve cell (neuron) connections in their brains.

Optimism is easily identified in brain scans. Levels of dopamine and other brain neurotransmitters rise, cortisol levels remain steady, and the amygdala is open and forwarding information to the prefrontal cortex. An optimistic state of mind enables a mindful response to stresses and a downplaying of thoughts of failure, frustration, and hopelessness. Optimism breeds the expectation of success, which in turn, makes it easier for the student to put forth the effort necessary to achieve that success.

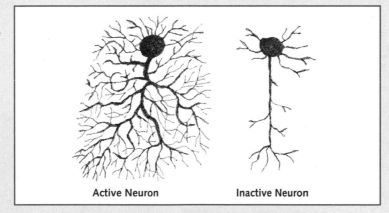

Active Neuron   Inactive Neuron

An active brain neuron, or nerve cell, forms many branching dendrites to make neural connections.

Clarify for the Class

Neuroplasticity allows us to train our brains, as we train our bodies to learn a sport. Explain that during brain training, repeated thoughts and experiences strengthen neural pathways, which, over time, come into play automatically. Similarly, when we train for a sport or practice playing an instrument, we strengthen body parts and create muscle memory through repetition.

Discuss: What is a specific physical task—basketball layups, a sequence of dance moves, rapid texting, and so on—that was difficult to learn at first? How did you improve that skill? Think of at least three challenging times during the school day when you can practice positive thinking to foster optimism. What can you do to help your brain work better?

Getting Ready

"Over" or "Under" Optimistic?
Hand gestures help show whether a thought is "over" (unrealistic), "under" (pessimistic), or "right in the middle" (optimistic).

GOALS

- Students will define optimistic and pessimistic mind-sets used to think about, react to, and approach a problem.
- Students will practice strategies that help them to develop and maintain optimism in their own lives.

MATERIALS

- chart paper
- copies of advice columns from newspapers or printed out from on-line sources (preview to make sure all problems are age-appropriate)
- (optional) Optimistic/Pessimistic/Unrealistic Thoughts activity sheet (p. 157)

CREATING THE OPTIMISTIC CLASSROOM

Classroom Management The strongest motivators for this age group are their peers. Ask students how they can help create a classroom culture that makes it okay to try and fail. You might ask them to come up with a class motto, such as: No mistakes = no learning. Ask students to share wise quotes, positive images, uplifting songs, and their own optimism. Suggested strategies:

- Invite students to post a "morning motivator" that will inspire their classmates for the day.
- Take a "motivation break" during a particularly complicated lesson.
- Encourage students to share success stories whenever appropriate.

Setting the Tone
Sharing funny stories is
one way to set a light
and optimistic tone in
the classroom.

MINDUP Warm-Up

Optimism: Over and Under

Explain that optimism doesn't mean pretending that everything is great when it is
not. Create a chart with three rows on the board. Label the top row "Unrealistic."
Label the middle row "Optimistic." Label the bottom row "Pessimistic." Then
brainstorm some situations that might cause students to worry, such as an upcoming
test, a school dance, a new school year, or a sick relative.

Take one situation and model the three kinds of responses for the class. Using the
example of an upcoming test, an unrealistic response might be, "I'll do great; I never
need to study." The optimistic response might be, "I'll give it my best effort and get
help if I need it; I'm confident I will be prepared." The pessimistic response might
be, "There's no point in studying; I'll just fail anyway—I always do." Have students
generate the three different responses to another situation.

Discuss: What do unrealistic and pessimistic thinking have in common? Which kind
of thinking is most likely to lead to action? Which kind of thinking is most likely to see
the world as all good or all bad? Which type of thinking gives you the most control
over the situation?

Leading the Lesson

Optimism in Training

Engage	Explore

What to Do

Ask students to reflect on the warm-up exercise. Get volunteers to offer a definition for optimism.

- What happens to your ability to solve problems when you are insufficiently optimistic?

- What happens to your ability to solve problems if you are overly optimistic?

Guide students to understand that optimistic thinking not only makes you happier, but also makes you a better problem solver. Pessimistic thinking leads you to feel discouraged and frustrated, and have little hope when faced with problems. Unrealistic thinking does not even acknowledge the problem.

Read these statements aloud (or create your own examples). Have students give a thumbs-up if they think the statement is optimistic and a thumbs-down if they think it is pessimistic or unrealistic.
"No swimming today! The rain spoiled everything."
"So what if it's raining? We can go to a movie instead."
"Forget about the weather. Let's just go swimming anyway."

Distribute copies of the advice column you pre-screened. Explain to students that they are going to hunt for examples of optimistic, pessimistic, and unrealistic thinking.

- Who can give an example of pessimistic thinking?

- Who can give an example of optimistic thinking?

- Was there any unrealistic thinking? If not, can you explain why?

Have students write out their ideas in the thought bubbles on the Optimistic/Pessimistic/Unrealistic Thoughts activity sheet.

- Which kind of thinking uses input from your prefrontal cortex?

- Which kind of thinking is influenced by the amygdala?

Why It's Important

This introduction helps students understand that optimistic thinking is a tool people can adopt.

NOTE: It is best to avoid labeling a person as "an optimist" or "a pessimist." We want students to think of optimism as a function of the brain's neuroplasticity, not as a hard-wired quality.

It's helpful to discuss optimism using the brain framework. Pessimistic and unrealistic thinking are influenced by the amygdala and shuts down higher-order thinking. The PFC gets more and clearer information from a calm amygdala, so works much better when problems are looked at realistically but with hope and confidence. Research shows that optimistic thinking makes people happier, healthier, and more successful in school and life.

From the Research
Mindfulness has been found to be related to well-being including optimism, positive affect, self-regulation, and lower rates of depression and anxiety.
(Brown & Ryan, 2003)

Reflect

Generate a class list of strategies students can use to adopt an optimistic perspective so their brain can stay healthy and work better.

- Considering other perspectives is one way to train your brain to think in a more open, positive way.

- What are some other ways to train your brain to think optimistically?

- How can you avoid a pessimistic or unrealistic way of thinking?

Record students' ideas on an "Our Best Ways to Stay Optimistic" class list that you can post in the room. Encourage students to keep a personal list as well. Ideas might include looking at another perspective on a problem, replacing a negative thought about something with a positive one, reminding ourselves that a worry is a feeling that can pass, doing a mindful breathing or sensing exercise, playing a game, singing a song, or sharing a joke.

This reflection should guide students to conclude that:
- Optimistic thinkers are happier, healthier, and more successful people.

- Optimistic thinking helps us to solve problems.

- We can choose to be optimistic and practice optimism so that it becomes a mind-set.

MINDUP
In the Real World

Career Connection

Although it may seem incongruous, hope and optimism often motivate medical researchers. Effective researchers are optimistic that a cure exists and believe that with enough patience and perseverance, determination and diligence, they will find a cure that will save thousands of lives. So often against all odds—working impossibly long hours with limited funds—medical researchers press on through endless samples and tests, hoping the next slide under the microscope will reveal the answer. What could be more optimistic than that?

Discuss: How might farmers, stockbrokers, and real estate developers depend on an optimistic outlook to conduct their work?

Once a Day

Before students leave for the period or the day, have them think of one thing they learned or enjoyed in class. Invite them to either tell it to you as they leave or write it on an "optimistic exit" card and hand it to you as they leave. This helps you assess what they have accomplished and highlights for them how they've benefitted from learning.

Connecting to the Curriculum

Learning about optimism supports students' connection to their own learning process and to the content areas and literature.

Journal Writing

Encourage your students to reflect on what they've learned about choosing optimism and to record questions to explore at another time. They may also enjoy responding to these prompts:

- Start a page with the words "Happiness is…." Make a list of as many things as you can think of. Return to your list whenever you think of something new to add. Return to it whenever you need a mood boost.

- Put one of your worries into perspective. In the first panel show the worst-case scenario. In the second panel show the best-case scenario. In the last panel, show the most likely scenario.

- Make a collage of goals. Try to depict goals that you have the power to accomplish—not like winning the lotto! You can use words and images to represent your goals. Put the collage in a place that is easily visible.

- Write your success story. Think of a time when you solved a problem, met a goal, or changed your attitude to be more optimistic. Explain what you accomplished, how you did it, and how it made you feel.

LANGUAGE ARTS
Comedy Sketch

What to Do
Pessimism and unrealistic optimism are staples of humor. Both kinds of thinking can create a gap between attitude and reality; the dissonance is often funny. Since students love to make each other laugh, give them the opportunity to work with a partner or a small group to come up with a comedy sketch about pessimism or unrealistic optimism.

What to Say
Work with a partner or a small group to come up with a funny scene that involves a character who is unrealistically optimistic or very pessimistic. The humor is in the character's inability to see the situation realistically. The tiny mouse that wants to fight an elephant is funny. The elephant scared of the mouse is also funny. Use these concepts to make your classmates laugh.

Why It's Important
One way to help students become more objective in their thinking is to show the humor in extreme thinking. Pessimistic thinking and unrealistic thinking are both very self-serious. Exposing both attitudes to humor helps deflate them. Laughter calms the amygdala and releases the PFC from the grip of emotion. Being able to laugh at oneself is a great remedy for distorted thinking.

SOCIAL STUDIES
Profiles in Optimism

What to Do
Explain to students that history is full of optimistic thinkers, who see possibility where others see problems. People often mistake them for unrealistic thinkers; if they were unrealistic, they wouldn't be able to see the obstacles and overcome them.

What to Say
Think of some of the people you've studied in social studies class. Think of people who explored new lands. Think of people who fought for freedom. Think of people who fought for justice. Think of people who overcame great odds. Choose someone who inspires you. Do some background research in the library or online and write a short biography of this person. Focus on how optimistic thinking was necessary to this person's success.

Why It's Important
Finding a role model from history helps them make a personal connection to what they are learning. Remaining optimistic in the face of serious challenges is inspiring, and finding inspiration helps foster optimism.

the Optimistic classroom™ journal

SCIENCE
Experiments in Optimism

What to Do
Point out that every scientific discovery has depended on optimistic thinking. Without optimistic thinking, no one would have the patience to study, observe, and test new hypotheses. Scientists must proceed with confidence as they commit themselves to doing something that hasn't been done before. Prepare some examples for students, such as the first suspension bridge, the polio vaccine, the lunar landing.

What to Say
All advances in science and technology come from optimistic thinking. Humans would still be sitting around waiting for a lightning strike to cook their food if they didn't have confidence in their own ability to make fire. Tell the story of an important discovery or advance. Focus on the role of optimism in the process. Explain the obstacles and how they were overcome.

Why It's Important
Science is often seen as a dry subject because it requires objectivity. However, the people responsible for the greatest advances were dreamers. They had to believe that what they were doing was possible, even if it had never been tried. This perspective will reinforce that optimism and problem solving go hand in hand.

SOCIAL-EMOTIONAL LEARNING
Opposite Mimes

What to Do
Have students generate a list of things that might lead to pessimistic thinking. Select a couple of scenarios that lend themselves to being acted out and assign each pair one of the scenarios. One partner will act out the scenario in a pessimistic way. The other will act it out in an optimistic way.

What to Say
Have you ever gotten pessimistic about doing a task? What about when your team was losing? What was your body language? What was your facial expression? Imagine going through the same scenario with an optimistic attitude. Practice acting out the scenario in silence. One partner will act it out pessimistically and the other will act it out optimistically.

Why It's Important
Students at this age are very concerned with their appearance and may be surprised at how clearly optimistic and pessimistic attitudes are communicated to others. Discuss how simple comportment choices like smiling can support optimism.

Literature Link
Drums, Girls, and Dangerous Pie

by Jordan Sonneblick
(2004). New York: Scholastic.

Steven Alper has typical problems. He likes a girl. He has an annoying younger brother. He has a typical wise-guy attitude. But his life soon gets a lot rougher when his younger brother is diagnosed with cancer. Suddenly, his attitude and how he responds to the new situation is no laughing matter.

Connect this book to the idea of finding the healthiest way to respond to difficult situations. Even when we can't control what is happening around us, we can still control ourselves.

More Books to Share

Gallo, Donald, ed. (2003). *Destination Unexpected.* Cambridge, MA: Candlewick Press.

Koertge, Ronald. (2006). *Shakespeare Bats Cleanup.* Cambridge, MA: Candlewick Press.

Ryan, Pam Muñoz. (2002). *Esperanza Rising.* New York: Scholastic.

the Optimistic classroom™ library

Appreciating Happy Experiences

What Does It Mean to Appreciate Happy Experiences?

We can make ourselves laugh over the memory of a hilarious situation shared with friends or flood ourselves with a feeling of warmth by recalling the hug of a beloved grandparent. To remember a happy experience fully and mindfully is to savor, or appreciate, it and reap the physical, emotional, and cognitive benefits.

Why Appreciate Happy Experiences?

Remembering a happy memory releases in our brain the same "feel-good" chemicals that flooded it at the time of the actual experience. We can practice mindfully recalling favorite memories as a strategy to achieve a variety of goals, including

- cultivating optimism
- alleviating negativity (e.g., boredom, sadness, worry)
- priming our brain for learning new material
- generating ideas from past experiences
- boosting our physical health

Students can learn to appreciate happy memories to help overcome specific negative feelings, such as sadness or insecurity. You can also integrate the concept into your teaching by creating learning experiences that are engaging and involve positive interactions and laughter, when possible. Those memories will be easy for students to recall and use as background support for classroom experiences.

What Can You Expect to Observe?

"It really helped to begin this practice by remembering a field trip we took. Combining our memories helped students elaborate. Then they tried it at home with friends and family. After a while, it became easier for students to call up good memories in detail."

—Sixth-grade teacher

Linking to Brain Research

Happy Memories Support a Can-Do Attitude

Recall from lessons 6 and 7 the critical role of the neurotransmitter most associated with pleasure, attention, reward, motivation, and perseverance—dopamine. Higher levels of dopamine in our brain result in feelings of hope, tolerance, motivation, and a can-do attitude—optimism. Dopamine release is triggered when we engage in pleasurable experiences like play-filled activities, laughing, physical exercise, acts of kindness, and positive social interactions.

Brain scans show that dopamine is released not only when we engage directly in pleasurable experiences, but also when we reflect on and remember these salient moments. In fact, remembering a positive experience can trigger dopamine release as powerfully as the real thing. By repeatedly referencing past successes, we build confidence and are more able to rebuff the "I can't" voice in our head. Happy memories can become a tool to prime the brain for new social, academic, and physical challenges.

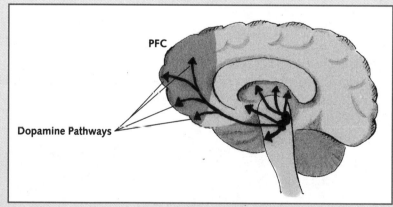

A major pathway of dopamine leads to the prefrontal cortex.

Clarify for the Class

Remembering a past success can refute thoughts of hopelessness and frustration. Explain that successful experiences trigger dopamine, which helps battle the "I can't" thoughts. Learning to recall achievements and reference past accomplishments applicable to a present dilemma can defuse panic and feelings of hopelessness. Write a journal entry about a goal you have, one you feel is a difficult challenge. Include memories of past successes related to your present challenge.

Discuss: How did you feel when you wrote about the challenge? Did you feel differently after remembering a related challenge that you had overcome or a task you had accomplished? What do you think happened in your brain when recalling the positive memory?

Getting Ready

Relaxing Recall
A smile lights the face of a student who's recalling a happy memory.

GOALS
- Students visualize and describe their thoughts, feelings, and physical sensations during a pleasurable experience.
- Students use recalling a pleasurable experience as a way to build optimism.

MATERIALS
- chart paper

CREATING THE OPTIMISTIC CLASSROOM

Brain-Inspired Instruction Each lesson you teach is an opportunity to create a pleasurable learning experience—not only as you teach it, but also as students reflect on it and savor it. Surefire dopamine boosters that enhance lessons include
- multimedia integration
- hands-on learning opportunities
- positive and supportive peer interaction
- personal emotional connections
- activity choices and opportunities to learn collaboratively

Sharing Memories
Students use a slide-show format to present their happy memory of a class field trip.

MINDUP Warm-Up

Memory-Sharing Practice

Think of something happy or funny that you and the class shared. Maybe there was an exciting field trip. Maybe you held the class outside. Maybe you had an interesting guest or presentation. Maybe someone told a good joke.

Invite students to build on this memory. The more you can elaborate, the more you all will be able to appreciate the memory. Think of the memory as a story and try to add important details. Encourage all students to participate. If details come up that are not as happy, acknowledge them as part of the experience but explain that you'd like to keep the focus on what was good.

Discuss: How did remembering something together help you savor the happiness of the memory? If an experience is less than perfect, how can we appreciate the good parts without feeling as if it was ruined? Does recalling a memory in detail change the way you feel? What is one of the main places in our brains where memories are stored?

Leading the Lesson

Memory Stretch and Savor

Engage	Explore

What to Do

Review the warm-up activity and relate remembering happy times to practicing optimism.

- One way to train our brains to think optimistically is to take time to enjoy happy memories we've had. To savor something is to appreciate it; we can savor the memory of an experience the same way we savor a delicious meal or a beautiful spring day.

- In this lesson, we're going to learn to remember mindfully—to savor a happy memory the way we savor a morsel of food during mindful tasting.

Give students time to write down notes of a happy memory, such as an adventure with a friend, a memorable field trip, or another exciting event. Instruct partners to tell their memory to each other. The listening partner should think of some questions to ask that will help deepen the description of the memory. Then give students time to make new notes.

- Did the questions your partner asked help you make your memory clearer?

- If so, what kind of new information did you add?

Let students know that they are going to spend some time savoring the memory they just finished stretching. Explain how appreciating their happy memory will be like making a mini-movie in their minds. Encourage them to close their eyes or look into their hands. You might begin and end the visualization by playing a tone on the resonant instrument you use for the Core Practice. Offer cues to help students fully visualize their happy experience.

- Bring all your attention to your happy experience.

- Start the mini-movie in your mind.

- See the place and the people involved.

- Remember nice things you heard and anything that smelled or tasted good.

- Linger on the good feelings in this memory.

- Notice how your body is feeling.

Why It's Important

Students may need some practice elaborating beyond simple expressions, such as "We played a fun game." They may need prompting to remember all the people involved, their expressions, the funny or meaningful actions they did, the role of weather, the details of setting, and so on. However, the exercise is likely to make them become better writers, as well as more optimistic people.

Providing plenty of structure and a quiet space for students to recall their memories will allow their amygdala to relax and their prefrontal cortex to receive and process all the input it's gathering.

Reflect

Give students time to share their experience of memory savoring.

- As you savored your memory, how did your brain feel? How did your body feel?

- What do you think was happening in your brain and body during the memory? How is that similar to or different from the mindful movement activity we did?

Help students understand that their brains can help change how they feel physically and emotionally—recalling happy memories is one way to do that.

Point out that while even happy memories may not be perfect, we can use them as a tool to feel better, to feel closer with friends and family, and to build optimistic thinking skills. Ask students to be very aware of happy moments that arise over the next few days. Remind them to capture the details so they can savor and revisit the happy feelings.

The experience of being flooded by warm emotions from a memory they choose provides students with proof that they can affect their own thoughts and feelings, even if they can't always control what happens around them. It also shows how quickly feelings can change—that students can improve their mood by a simple mindful practice that takes about a minute to complete.

MINDUP
In the Real World

Career Connection

Pleasure may begin with our ability to notice and relish details—appreciation for the hands that made a tasty soup, enjoyment of a shared song, and deep satisfaction of a handmade gift. One of the joys of being around young children is their natural ability to appreciate the smallest details of an experience. A prekindergarten teacher will often witness with a sense of wonder and delight—splashing in a rain puddle, watching a butterfly or playing with shadows on a wall as she or he sees the world through the eyes of young children. Spending time with young children allows us to pay attention to the small events that are ours to appreciate too.

Discuss: How is it that *all* careers offer opportunities to savor happiness? Give an example of how a person can find enjoyment on the job, even when it's stressful or difficult.

Once a Day

Teach to create a happy memory, whether you incorporate humor, a song, a game, or some other kind of positive group interaction. Learning like this creates memories that are easy for students to recall and for you to build new instruction on.

Connecting to the Curriculum

Appreciating happy experiences supports students' connection to their own learning process and to the content areas and literature.

Journal Writing

Encourage your students to reflect on what they've learned about appreciating happy experiences and to record questions to explore at another time. They may also enjoy responding to these prompts:

- Keep a happy memory journal. Start writing down things that make you happy during the day. See if you can add enough details so you can picture it again in your mind later.

- Interview a friend or a family member about one of his or her happiest memories with you. Write down or record what they say to use as a mood-booster when you need one.

- Write down a plan for a future happy memory. Try to plan something small enough to do without a lot of time, money, or effort. If it happens, go back and compare your plan to what happened.

- Write a letter to someone you shared a happy memory with. Fill it with details that show you remember it well. Tell the person why the memory means so much to you.

LANGUAGE ARTS
Write What You Know

What to Do
Many writers mine their memories when elaborating the rich details that create a believable world for their stories. However, their memories of an experience may be far from the original experience itself. Challenge students to play with their memories and use them loosely. Encourage them to use their memories as a jumping-off point.

What to Say
A famous motto among writers is "write what you know." That means that writers often use their memories to inspire them. You can do that, too. Write a story based on a memory. You don't need to write exactly what happened. You can make up characters and change the setting. Remember to fill your story with details, just as you did when you were savoring your memory.

Why It's Important
Getting students to elaborate in their writing is often a big challenge. Anyone who has ever asked a middle-schooler about his or her day is familiar with a flair for terse descriptions. So it makes sense to leverage the elaboration work they did on their memories and apply it to writing. You can suggest that students reuse the strategy of having a partner ask questions, if they find it helpful.

SCIENCE
Memory-Mood Experiments

What to Do
Scientists are still studying how memory works. Invite students to join this process by devising their own experiments. Have students work in groups to come up with an experiment that can test ideas about memory and mood. Arrange to have each group use the other groups as their test subjects and vice versa. Then give them time to talk about the results and see what conclusions they draw.

What to Say
Is it easier to remember the good or the bad? Let's test that. For example, if you have two lists of words (one positive, one negative), is one list easier to remember? What if you had the same list of words, but showed people a happy or sad picture with it? Come up with an original experiment that you can test here in the class. Try to use the data to form a conclusion.

Why It's Important
Devising their own experiments teaches students about what does and doesn't work as an investigation, and what constitutes a "successful" experiment.

SOCIAL STUDIES
Sourcing Memories

What to Do

Discuss with students the concept of a primary source and contrast it with a secondary source. They should understand that a primary source includes any material that was involved in the original event or generated by one of its participants. They should also understand that a secondary source is a record of the event created later by someone who was not present.

What to Say

Let's brainstorm different primary sources. They include records, such as text messages, flyers, pictures, and weather reports. They also include objects, such as articles of clothing or trophies. Assemble or describe as many primary sources as you can for a happy memory. Then swap with a partner who will interview you and try to create a secondary-source account of your memory. See how well your partner describes what happened.

Why It's Important

This activity will help clarify for students what constitutes a primary source and appreciate their tremendous variety. Understanding how historians create secondary sources from primary sources will help students connect to the underlying work of historians and also help them put their history textbooks into perspective!

SOCIAL-EMOTIONAL LEARNING
Scrapping Class

What to Do

Share an example of a scrapbook with artifacts, pointing out that these artifacts are all primary sources. Set up a station in class where students create scrapbook pages of primary-source artifacts. Add to the album each month.

What to Say

Scrapbooking is a good way to savor happy memories. Let's be on the lookout for primary-source artifacts to put in a class book. Which artifacts help us best remember the good times and good feelings we shared? How can we display and really savor them?

Why It's Important

Creating a class scrapbook creates strong bonds inside the classroom community, based on shared experiences. It gives you, the teacher, impetus to plan events that students will want to capture and remember.

Literature Link
Confetti Girl

by Diana López
(2009). New York: Scholastic.

Why would anyone collect socks? Lina has her own way of doing things and this quality helps her deal with the ups and downs of middle school. Students will enjoy discovering how Lina's sense of humor, *dichos* (proverbs) she learned from her parents, and her ability to remember happy times help face new challenges, such as feeling left out when her best friend becomes more interested in boys that anything else.

More Books to Share

Danticat, Edwidge. (2002). *Behind the Mountains* (First Person Fiction). New York: Scholastic.

Ho, Minfong. (2003). *The Stone Goddess* (First Person Fiction). New York: Scholastic.

Veciana-Suarez, Ana. (2004). *Flight to Freedom* (First Person Fiction). New York: Scholastic.

the Optimistic classroom™ library

Taking Action
Mindfully

Learning to express gratitude and perform acts of kindness helps children build the awareness, cognitive skills, compassion, and confidence to contribute in a meaningful way to the classroom and the world.

Lesson 13:
Expressing Gratitude... 126

Children gain an appreciation for special people and things in their lives and discover the social, emotional, and cognitive benefits of showing gratitude.

Lesson 14:
Performing Acts of Kindness 134

As children perform small acts of kindness for friends, classmates, teachers, and family, they learn how these positive actions can increase their optimism and brain power.

Lesson 15:
Taking Mindful Action in the World............... 142

Children collaboratively plan and perform a group act of kindness and reflect on the way combined efforts can make an important difference in the world and connect them to their peers and the larger community.

"When you give yourself, you receive more than you give." The lessons in this unit give credence to Saint-Exupéry's famous quote. Certainly, there are obvious benefits for the recipients of kind actions children will do in these lessons—from helping lift a classmate's spirits to raising funds for victims of a natural disaster on the other side of the world. Yet participating mindfully in positive social actions can affect children's social, emotional, and cognitive growth in transformational ways.

By expressing gratitude and performing acts of kindness, children develop a stronger understanding of the feelings of other people and a concern for the well-being of others. Research shows that actions that engender feelings of empathy and compassion have a number of positive benefits, such as boosting the production of the feel-good neurotransmitter dopamine, increasing the likelihood that children will continue to act on their social concerns, and improving their capacity to take care of themselves.

Expressing Gratitude

What is Gratitude?

Gratitude is a feeling of thankfulness and joy we feel in response to something we've received, whether the gift is tangible, such as a book we look forward to reading, or intangible, such as a smile of encouragement from a loved one or a breathtaking view of a landscape.

Why Practice Expressing Gratitude?

Simply focusing for a minute on the experiences in our lives we're grateful for shifts our thinking to a calmer, more contented perspective, which can immediately uplift and comfort us. When we make the expression of gratitude a regular practice—whether we make a daily written list or a mental tally of things we're grateful for as we start or end each day—we train our brain to shift to a positive mind-set more efficiently and maintain a healthier, more optimistic perspective.

This lesson gives students the opportunity to identify and share with peers expressions of gratitude for people, events, and things in their lives. This sharing forges stronger connections and trust among peers. The mindful listening required in the lesson also cultivates students' empathy, laying the foundation for planning and performing acts of kindness over the course of the final two lessons.

What Can You Expect to Observe?

"Some students worried that they would run out of things to be grateful for. But we found out that the more you look for opportunities to be thankful, the more you find. Expressing gratitude makes us all feel very fortunate, and I see students becoming more generous as a result."

—Sixth-grade teacher

Linking to Brain Research

The Many Gifts of Gratitude

Gratitude has powerful physiological effects on the brain—and body. Researchers have found that when we think about someone or something we truly appreciate, our bodies calm themselves. The feelings that come with gratitude trigger the calming branch of the autonomic nervous system, the parasympathetic system. The sympathetic system is the "fight, flight, or freeze" responder during emergencies, stress, and intense activity. The counteracting parasympathetic system is all about "rest and digest." It slows the heartbeat, shunts blood from the muscles to the organs, and contracts the pupils of the eyes. Feeling appreciative also produces a more even heart rhythm, which may reduce the risk of heart attacks and relieve hypertension.

Feeling thankful and appreciative also affects levels of brain neurotransmitters, including releasing dopamine toward the prefrontal cortex where reasoning and logic occur. Dopamine not only fosters contentment, it is also the main player in the brain's reward and motivation system. Experiments have shown that those who keep gratitude journals or lists feel more optimistic and make more progress toward their goals. And young people who do daily self-guided exercises in gratitude have higher levels of alertness, enthusiasm, determination, attentiveness, and energy (Emmons & McCullough). Students who practice grateful thinking not only have a more positive attitude toward school, their brains are more ready to learn.

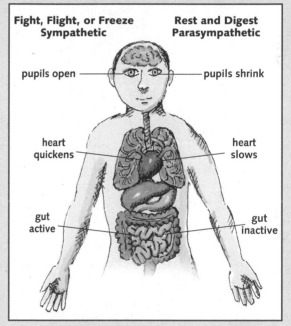

The autonomic nervous system has two parts: sympathetic and parasympathetic.

Clarify for the Class

Explain the differences between the stress-fueled sympathetic system and the relaxing parasympathetic system of the body's autonomic nervous system. Students can easily observe one of these functions—pupil dilation—because it also works to adjust the amount of light entering the eye. Have pairs of students take turns standing near a bright window or light and noticing how the opening of each other's pupils automatically shrinks, or contracts, in bright light and grows, or dilates, in low light.

Discuss: Which system do you think is triggered when practicing gratitude—the "fight, flight, or freeze" sympathetic system or the "rest and digest" parasympathetic system? What triggers the sympathetic system for you?

Getting Ready

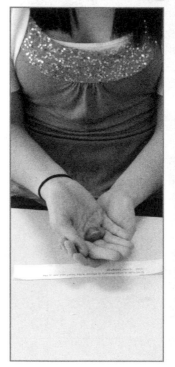

Props for Gratitude
A special prop that has a calming quality, like a feather, a polished stone, or necklace beads, can be passed around a gratitude circle.

GOALS
- Students learn the meaning of gratitude and the importance of expressing gratitude.
- Students identify things in their life for which they are grateful.

MATERIALS
- chart paper
- bowl of beads (these can be made by students from clay or rolled paper)
- string (be sure it's narrow enough to fit through beads)

CREATING THE OPTIMISTIC CLASSROOM
Supporting English Language Learners Help students with limited English language skills participate in the sharing part of the lesson in one of several ways:

- Allow students to sketch the object(s) of their gratitude and write a short caption.
- Offer students the opportunity to write about their gratitude in their first language and then translate their thoughts into English.
- Give students a frame for participating in the circle, such as "I am grateful for _____ because _____." Students at higher levels can explain why they are grateful, while students at a beginner level might share the one word or idea.
- Invite students to teach the class to say "Thank you" in their home language.

Grateful Words
Students enjoy sharing and
discussing famous quotations
that express gratitude.

MINDUP Warm-Up

Gratitude Practice

Ask students to take a deep breath and think of positive things that others have done
for them recently or that they have done for others. As students share, ask the class
to put these things into categories, such as polite gestures (e.g., saving a seat), kind
words (e.g., cheering someone up), kind acts (e.g., sharing a snack), gifts, favors
(e.g., helping with homework), and volunteering or donating to charity.

On scratch paper have students list all the ways you can show gratitude, such as
feeling quietly grateful, saying "Thank you," writing a letter, sending a card or e-card,
calling someone, sending an email or text, or doing something nice in return. What
other ways of expressing gratitude can they think of?

Discuss: Which are the best ways to thank someone in the different categories?
Does how well you know the person matter? Does the amount of money or effort
matter? How do you decide? Explain that there are no right or wrong answers.
However, in some cases, how we say "Thank you" is governed by etiquette. For
example, sending a note expressing gratitude for a gift is considered polite behavior.

Leading the Lesson

Wear Your Gratitude

Engage

What to Do

Have students recall from the Warm-Up activity how and why we express our thanks. Remind students also of the happiness-savoring exercise, in case they want to express gratitude for whatever made them happy. Provide other examples that everyone can claim, such as a sunny day, the chance to learn new things, and spending time with people you love.

- Today, I'd like you to start by thinking of three things that you're grateful for.

- Then we'll use beads as symbols we can wear on a bracelet or necklace.

Encourage students to offer gratitude only for things that cannot be purchased from a store. Let them know that experts who have studied happiness (the field is called positive psychology) say that we get more joy from experiences than from objects.

Why It's Important

This exercise can help give students a better sense of perspective about themselves. Students at this age can be emotionally fragile and less than completely self-assured. They may focus on flaws that they see magnified out of proportion. Some students have adult problems that they are not yet prepared to handle. Focusing on what is good in their lives can help provide a counterbalance when things feel overwhelming.

Explore

What to Do

Give everyone a length of string. Let them measure it on themselves, either as a bracelet, necklace, or something they can keep in their pocket. Remind them to leave some extra for tying a knot. The bowl of beads will be passed around three times. Each person can take one bead each pass.

- When you receive the bowl of beads, you may name something you are grateful for, and then pass the bowl to the next person.

- Please listen mindfully, without commenting on what that person says.

- If you choose not to say anything, hold the bead in your hand, think your thought of gratitude and pass it along.

Congratulate students for sharing and listening mindfully.

For the next few days, have them keep a journal in which they will record how they feel whenever their beads remind them of their gratitude. You may have them keep a separate Gratitude Journal or use their MindUP Journal.

Why It's Important

Providing two different modes for students to express their thoughts of gratitude (group circle and journal) offers students a chance to hear and appreciate the thoughts of their classmates and to present their own ideas safely. Establishing the no-comments rule will increase students' sense of security in sharing, as will the option to express the thought silently. (See the box on page 130 for ways to support ELLs.)

From the Research

. . . by experiencing gratitude, a person is motivated to carry out prosocial behavior, energized to sustain moral behaviors, and inhibited from committing destructive interpersonal behaviors.
(McCullough et al., 2001)

Reflect

After a few days of keeping notes, invite students to discuss their experience with the gratitude practices.

- How did your beads affect your mood? What did you notice about your thinking?

- How was sharing in the circle? What was it like to talk about your gratitude out loud and hear what others had to say?

Build on students' responses to help them recognize the positive effects that gratitude practices can have, such as improving our mood, helping us think more clearly, connecting us with the people and things we're grateful for, connecting us with others who are expressing gratitude, and giving us a sense of well-being or happiness.

Plan with students how they can make gratitude journal writing and gratitude circle sharing a daily or weekly practice to add to their tool kit.

Cognitive research suggests that when people focus on the things they are grateful for, their happiness increases. Making a habit of expressing gratitude helps us be mindful about the important things in life and focus on the bigger picture, leading to a greater appreciation for other people and the larger world around us. Consider the best format and give students a say in helping you design a plan for integrating gratitude into the school day.

MINDUP
In the Real World

Career Connection

Feeling grateful enables people in any circumstance to relax and experience a sense of peace and happiness. That's especially important when the type of task a person is doing is stressful, such as working late to meet a deadline, or tiring, such as spending many hours standing or sitting. One way to generate feelings of gratitude and find ways to do the work at hand even better is to seek feedback from coworkers and supervisors. When we receive genuine, constructive criticism from people whose goal is to help us do our job better, we discover new ways to do tasks or solve problems—and that is something to be grateful for!

Discuss: Constructive criticism from other people helps us see our work from a different or more experienced perspective. This often gives us a new way to approach a problem or simplify a task. Think of a time when feedback from others has helped you improve.

Once a Day

Seek feedback from a colleague or student on the way you explain a concept, lead a routine, or implement a strategy you'd like help improving. Consider the way the perceptions and ideas of others can plant the seeds of growth.

Connecting to the Curriculum

Journal Writing

Encourage your students to reflect on what they've learned about expressing gratitude and to record questions to explore at another time. They may also enjoy responding to these prompts:

- Think of a nice thing that somebody once did for you. How can you pass it on? Make a plan and then a progress report.

- Sometimes you can find something small to be grateful for, even within a problem. Write a poem about finding a silver lining in a dark cloud.

- Do a drawing or make a collage about things in nature that you are grateful for. Hang it where you can see it every day.

- Write a thank-you letter to someone who makes you happy. The letter doesn't have to be about anything this person did. Just let the person know how much you appreciate his or her presence in your life.

SOCIAL STUDIES
Amazing Technology

What to Do
Before the industrial revolution, all work had to be done by hand. The only "power" was the strength of an animal, which is why an engine's power is still described as horsepower. Steam engines caused a revolution in transportation and manufacturing. Computers and their networks changed our lives again. Point out that technological advances are not evenly distributed in the world, and that many people today live as they always have.

What to Say
Think about all the technology you use today. Write a letter to someone in the past about the kind of "superpowers" today's technology gives people. First you must make a list of some of the most impressive technologies. Then you should break down into simple terms what they do. Try to show some understanding of how things could be accomplished without this technology.

Why It's Important
Understanding how technology has changed our lives will help students begin to picture how people lived in the past without it. Students will also begin to appreciate some of the advantages of living in a developed nation.

MATH
Charting Life Expectancy

What to Do
People are often grateful for good health. One way to measure the health of a society is to look at life expectancy. Have students choose an inquiry, such as life expectancy across history or around the world. Provide materials or instruct students to do research in the library or online. Have students present their findings as a graph.

What to Say
Life expectancy is a statistic that measures the general health of a population. Violence, disease, and lack of nutrition can all reduce life expectancy. Which populations would you like to investigate? What information are you going to look for? Graph your findings and present them to the class.

Why It's Important
This activity will give students practice making visual representations of data, an important skill. It will also remind students that they have been born into a very fortunate time and place.

the Optimistic classroom™ journal

SCIENCE
One and Only Earth?

What to Do

Have students generate a list of all the elements and systems we depend upon for survival here on Earth. Organize students into groups that will explore how each supports human life. Encourage students to come up with a visual display, such as a Web diagram showing the many ways humans benefit from this system. They might use sketches, images found online, or magazine photos to enhance their work. Have groups share their presentations.

What to Say

Scientists are always looking for planets with attributes that are similar to Earth. What kinds of things would support us? Think beyond the air and water. Think about the atmosphere, the climate, the amount of gravity. Choose an attribute of Earth that is necessary for life. Explain how it works and why it is important. After the presentations we can talk about the likelihood of finding another Earth.

Why It's Important

This activity helps students recognize how essential our planet, which we tend to take for granted, is to our health and survival. That understanding gives students a sense of connection to Earth, provides imaginative fuel for the possibilities of space colonies in the future, and helps students expand their gratitude list.

SOCIAL-EMOTIONAL LEARNING
Gratitude Slogans

What to Do

It's easy to take things for granted, and it requires effort to keep an attitude of appreciation. Have the class work on slogans of gratitude that you can post or use as occasional reminders. Remind students to apply what they have learned about being thankful. Encourage them to be playful.

What to Say

Have you ever heard the saying "An apple a day keeps the doctor away"? Well, how about this: "A 'thank-you' a day keeps the blues away"? Let's come up with more of our own slogans to post and use in class to remind us to appreciate the good things we have.

Why It's Important

Making students partners in how the class practices gratitude increases the likelihood they'll engage in the practice on their own; self-initiating the practice cultivates mindful thinking and encourages students to self-regulate their behaviors and take good emotional care of themselves.

Literature Link
Esperanza Rising

by Pam Munoz Ryan
(2000). New York: Scholastic.

Esperanza was a girl who had everything. She had a rich family who loved her. One day her whole world comes crashing down. Her father is murdered. She must move to the United States and become a poor worker. Will Esperanza find anything left to be grateful for?

Connect this book to the idea that material wealth is not all there is in life to be grateful for. As students read they will see how the character grows and changes.

More Books to Share

Bly, Robert. (2008). *Count Your Blessings: 63 Things To Be Grateful For In Everyday Life…And How To Appreciate Them.* Nashville, TN: Thomas Nelson Publishing.

Peck, R. (2009). *A Season Of Gifts.* New York: Dial.

Roberts, Cynthia. (2007). *Thankfulness.* Mankato, MN: Child's World.

the Optimistic classroom™ library

Performing Acts of
Kindness

What Are Acts of Kindness?

Good deeds … gestures of generosity … paying it forward. These expressions describe mindful action intended to help another living being. Participating in such an action constitutes an act of kindness. Acts of kindness can be big or small, spontaneous or well planned.

Why Perform Acts of Kindness?

Think back to a time when someone helped you out unexpectedly or gave you a compliment. Memories like this have intense staying power (in fact, they may be part of a larger happy memory) and often remind us that we can act in the same way to help, encourage, or comfort someone else. Socially, acts of kindness cultivate shared happiness, build relationships, and give people a sense of connectedness to a group, community, or place— they are an excellent way to build a classroom community full of good will and optimism.

In this lesson, students plan several acts of kindness, which not only benefit the larger community but also help develop the neural networks that build students' sense of compassion and empathy. The more people practice acts of kindness, the more likely they are to recognize and act on situations in which others are in need.

What Can You Expect to Observe?

"My students have discovered the 'helper's high' and we have been having a lot of fun with it. It began with exaggerated gestures of doors being held open with a flourish, and students trying to outdo each other with compliments. But it is beginning to take root in earnest because it makes everyone feel good."

—Seventh-grade teacher

Linking to Brain Research

Our Brains Are Built for Compassion and Empathy

Being concerned about the welfare of others and understanding the feelings of those around us are basic skills for emotional intelligence. Compassion and empathy can be developed through mindfully practicing acts of kindness. As children develop compassion and empathy, they learn to recognize that their words and actions have an impact on others. This feeling of interconnectedness helps them reflect on their responses to the words and actions of others and better monitor and control their emotional responses. Practicing compassion and empathy builds the social and emotional competence that children need in order to be resilient and confident

Brain research studies confirm the power of practicing kindness. Brain scans reveal that neural pathways involved in detecting emotions are dramatically strengthened in people with extensive, focused experiences in practicing compassion. Other studies have shown that our brains are rewarded for altruism with a release of dopamine during acts of kindness. We are hard-wired to feel good about doing good.

Scientists are discovering that compassion is an emotion as evolutionarily ancient as fear or anger. Brain scans of subjects feeling compassion while watching videos of strangers in despair and grief show activity not only in the higher brain's cortex but also in the hypothalamus and brain stem.

Clarify for the Class

Human brains are hard-wired for altruism. Explain that altruism is behavior that benefits someone else rather than oneself. Our brains release the feel-good neurotransmitter dopamine in response to altruistic acts. This reinforces feelings of interconnectedness.

Discuss: What are some examples of altruistic acts? Have you ever felt better after doing an altruistic act? What do you think happened in your brain? Why do you think the brain is hard-wired to make humans feel good about doing good?

Getting Ready

Greetings That Keep 'Em Smiling
Find routines like a special before-class greeting that allow you to recognize and make a unique connection with each student.

GOALS
- Students find three opportunities to show kindness and perform three acts of kindness.
- Students explore the benefits—for themselves and for others— of being kind.

MATERIALS
- chart paper
- index cards

CREATING THE OPTIMISTIC CLASSROOM
Classroom Management Allow your students to help you develop a culture of kindness in the classroom. Discuss different types of classroom behaviors and rate them together on a kindness scale. Use these ratings to generate a rubric of kind classroom behavior. Once you have developed this with everyone's participation, treat it as a social contract. Let the students know that you will hold them to their standards. This will work even better if you will allow yourself to be held to the same.

Polite Acts = Mindful Acts
Holding the door for another
or making room for others in a
group space is a way for students
to be mindful of the presence of
people around them.

MIND̂UP Warm-Up

Kindness Practice

Challenge the class to come up with some compliments for themselves as a group.
Have them finish the sentence stem: "We are a class that…." Students can also
finish that stem in an aspirational way; for example, "We are a class that strives to be
kind." (Remind students to keep compliments focused on positive effort or behavior
and avoid commenting on physical appearances or material possessions.)

Have each student write his or her name on an index card and put it in a container.
Ask students to pick a card at random and keep the name on it a secret. Within a
designated time frame (a school period or day), task students with performing an act
of kindness for that student. No money should be spent. Tell students to notice any
act of kindness done for them. Tell them to try to witness as many acts of kindness
being done by their classmates as they can.

Discuss: Have students report the kindness that was done for them and any they
noticed. Discuss which felt better—receiving an act of kindness, performing one, or
noticing one. Discuss what an act of kindness looks like. How do you recognize it
when you see it?

Leading the Lesson

Kindness Scavenger Hunt

Engage

What to Do

Review the Warm-Up exercise to focus students' attention on what kindness means and the ways in which it is already part of their life experience.

- Does it have to take a lot of time to be kind?

- Does it have to cost you anything to be kind?

- Do you need special expertise to be kind?

- Who deserves our kindness?

- How do you feel after you've done something kind?

- How do you feel after you've witnessed an act of kindness?

Have students talk in pairs to come up with a definition of kindness. Work with the class to synthesize a definition, such as "Kindness is a mindful choice to act in a friendly, helpful way toward others."

Explore

Connect kindness to gratitude, optimism, and perspective taking.

- When you feel optimistic, are you more or less likely to act kindly?

- Could performing an act of kindness cause you to feel grateful? Could being grateful cause you to perform an act of kindness?

- Was there a time when seeing the way someone else felt (seeing their perspective) helped you perform an act of kindness that noticeably benefited that person?

Announce a kindness scavenger hunt. Have students brainstorm a list of kind actions they might perform, such as saying hello to a new student, assisting a peer with a challenging assignment, inviting someone who looks left out to join their group, and appreciating someone's hard work. Have them check off any action on the list that they performed. Leave a space marked "Other" for ideas not on the original list.

Why It's Important

This discussion helps students understand that acting on kindness is something that doesn't have to involve lots of money or time and that simple kindness can take many forms. It is helpful to review examples of kindness—giving compliments, picking up litter, holding a door, saving a seat, lending a pen, and so on.

Making connections among the concepts students have been learning and practicing may help them see how this positive, brain-building work all fits together. Students who are more mature may be more able than younger students to grasp the role of perspective taking in acting kindly; this is a concept to emphasize and repeat.

Reflect

After a day's time, gather students together to reflect on their experiences during their kindness scavenger hunt. Put them with partners to talk about their most memorable act of kindness.

Then ask volunteers to share. Help students make connections by having them revisit the questions you asked before their brainstorming.

- Did anyone experience an optimistic feeling before or after their act of kindness?

- What role did gratitude play in your act of kindness?

- Before you performed your act, did you use perspective taking to understand what might help someone?

Help students understand the importance of being kind and the positive impact of kindness on the brain.

This reflection should guide students to conclude that:

- Helping others can improve our mood and make us feel connected with other people and things.

- Kindness, optimism, and gratitude reinforce one another.

- Acts of kindness can boost our brain power and help us see the bigger picture in our lives.

MINDUP
In the Real World

Career Connection

Those who bring sunshine to the lives of others cannot keep it from themselves, wrote J.M. Barrie, the author of *Peter Pan.* It is one of life's mysteries that a gift that costs nothing rewards the giver with both happiness and health—that gift, of course, is kindness. Performing acts of kindness has been shown to boost the positive energy of all involved, both the one who gives *and* the one who receives. The Center for Compassion and Altruism Research and Education at the Stanford University School of Medicine aims to conduct scientific research on the neural underpinnings of kindness, altruism, and compassion: What happens to your brain when its focus is on kindness?

Discuss: What are some service learning projects older kids you know are involved in? How are acts of kindness a part of the tasks participants are assigned?

Once a Day

Reach out professionally and personally to colleagues. Share a creative teaching tip, remember a birthday, and build a more supportive and cohesive work environment.

Connecting to the Curriculum

Performing acts of kindness supports students' connection to their own learning process and to the content areas and literature.

Journal Writing

Encourage your students to reflect on what they've learned about doing kind actions and to record questions to explore at another time. They may also enjoy responding to these prompts:

- Count acts of kindness for a week. Write down all the acts of kindness you do, all you witness, and any acts of kindness that were done for you. After a week, look back at your entries. What do you notice?

- Perform a secret act of kindness. Can you do it without anyone noticing or giving you credit for it? Write a paragraph describing the experience and whether or not you were successful. How did it feel?

- Design an award for the kindest act you have ever witnessed or experienced. What impressed you about this act? Why would you rank it above the others?

- Make a public service announcement (PSA) for kindness. Why should people try to be kinder? How will you persuade them?

SCIENCE
Kindness in the Kingdom

What to Do
Set up the concept of animal altruism. Explain that kindness is a human trait because we choose to be kind. However, there is such a thing as altruism among animals. This is when animals do something good for the group that may not be so good for the individual. Provide resources for students to investigate this topic, or provide time for them to use the library or Internet.

What to Say
Why would animals be altruistic and do something that has an advantage for their group but a disadvantage for them as individuals? Find an example in the animal kingdom of animals that behave altruistically. How do their actions benefit the group? Why are these actions not beneficial to the individual? What is at risk? Present your findings back to the class.

Why It's Important
Students will learn that animal altruism is an important trait for survival among animals that live in groups. This may explain why our brains reward us for behaving in altruistic ways. However, as humans we have awareness that lets us choose how we behave, while animals are more likely operating out of instinct.

LANGUAGE ARTS
Stories of Kindness

What to Do
Prepare students for a read-aloud of the O. Henry story "The Gift of the Magi." You may pre-teach some of the difficult vocabulary or explain it as you read. Give students some background before you read. Explain that this is the story of a young couple who don't have much money but want to give each other a special present.

What to Say
What do you think about the ending of this story: Is it happy or is it sad? The gift giving didn't work out very well, but they each got something that money could not buy. Work in groups to come up with a modern-day version of the story. Then you can read your version to the class.

Why It's Important
This classic story offers students the opportunity to apply their prior knowledge of kindness to understanding a text. They can make inferences about the characters' motivations and feelings.

Literature Link
Dear Miss Breed

by Joanne Oppenheim
(2006). New York: Scholastic.

During World War II, when Japanese Americans were being sent to interment camps, one librarian refused to forget her patrons. She sent letters and care packages with books and other gifts. At a terrible time in the country's history, Miss Breed's kindness stood out.

Connect this story to students' own kindness practice. Discuss how difficult conditions can make kindness rarer and also more necessary.

More Books to Share

Acts of Kindness/Inspirational Stories of Kindness at www.actsofkindness.org/stories.

Deedy, C. (2009). *14 Cows for America*. Atlanta: Peachtree.

Peck, R. (2009). *A Season of Gifts*. New York: Dial.

SOCIAL STUDIES
History's Kindest Heroes

What to Do
List some examples of kindness in history, such as the Native Americans who helped starving pilgrims, the Europeans who hid and fed victims of the Holocaust, the white people who participated in the Abolition and the Civil Rights movements, or the 9/11 heroes who went into the Twin Towers to save others.

What to Say
Which examples of kindness in history do you find the most powerful? Work with students who are interested in the same historic moment. Use the Internet or library resources to find specific stories of kindness to share with the class. Gather plenty of details so that the class can be inspired by your story about these heroes.

Why It's Important
This activity connects concepts of kindness, perspective taking, and optimism to students' understanding of different historical moments. It offers role models for them as they expand their understanding of social responsibility beyond the classroom.

SOCIAL-EMOTIONAL LEARNING
Book of Kindness

What to Do
Make a class book to record acts of kindness. Create a blank page template that has four labeled sections: 1. Kindness Performed, 2. Kindness Received, 3. Kindness Witnessed, and 4. Comments on Kindness. One student may begin a page, filling in one section, and post it for peers to complete.

What to Say
Each act of kindness can be recorded from multiple perspectives: the perspective of the person who performed the act, that of the person who received the kindness, that of someone who witnessed the act, and that of a person reading the account. What can we learn from all these different perspectives?

Why It's Important
A class book of acts of kindness is another document, like the scrapbook of memories, that shows students' growing sense of community. It also reinforces their sense of social responsibility, as they make additions to the book and then read different perspectives on each event.

the Optimistic classroom™ library

Taking Mindful Action in the World

What Are Mindful Actions?

Whether they involve one or many individuals, mindful actions are purposefully planned activities that create a healthier, happier world and set a precedent for other people to follow. You might say that mindful actions take acts of kindness to the world beyond the classroom.

Why Reach Beyond the Classroom?

At this point in their MindUp learning journey, students have a range of optimism-building strategies to call on. They are beginning to feel confident in their ability to monitor and nurture themselves and to be receptive to the perspectives and needs of others. They are ready to expand their kindness practice to create a bigger "ripple effect" in their world.

In this culminating lesson, students work together to select, plan, and execute a group act of kindness for the school, community, or world. Through actions like this, students are able to see themselves as part of a larger context—they glimpse the big picture of the world around them, and link their own peace of mind to a more generalized sense of peace. Their role as active participants in building that community fosters a sense of comfort, belonging, and optimism and increases their desire to make thoughtful, ethical decisions both independently and with others.

What Can You Expect to Observe?

"Many students are excited to make a difference in the 'real world' outside of school. Their enthusiasm is great enough to jump hurtles that would stop many adults. Finding outlets for this wonderful energy will benefit us all."

—Sixth-grade teacher

Linking to Brain Research

Mirror Neurons:
Kindness Is Contagious!

Research on mirror neurons is helping us understand the power of social interactions and connections. Mirror neurons are a kind of brain nerve cell that allows the brain to imitate the actions of others, and also to feel the emotions experienced by others. Our pain receptors flinch (as does our body) when we see someone stub a toe. Our amygdala relaxes when we see a mother gently rocking her baby. The neural pathways associated with specific emotions such as pain, joy, and fear are activated when we see a face expressing that emotion.

When a group works together in a positive way—specifically, through altruism—feelings of kindness, levels of dopamine, and opportunities for activating the neural pathways of pleasure and reward multiply. This makes kindness "contagious." Recent studies show that individuals who belong to social groups that focus on kindness and altruism have higher levels of dopamine, and more empathy and compassion. As we engage in acts of kindness and are emotionally rewarded for it, our need to be kind becomes a deciding factor in our choice of words and actions.

Mirror neurons in certain regions of the brain activate in an identical manner both during an emotional experience and when seeing someone else have that emotional experience.

Clarify for the Class

Explain that special nerve cells called mirror neurons help our brains understand the feelings of, or have empathy for, other people. Practicing compassion strengthens the neural pathways for detecting emotions in others. Have small groups of students share stories about a minor hurt, such as getting a shot at the doctor's office or getting a paper cut in school. Ask them to pay attention to how each story makes them feel.

Discuss: Did you feel your body flinch during the stories? Did you think about a time when something similar happened to you? What do you think was happening in your brain when you heard these stories? How do empathy and compassion help us interact with family and friends and live in a society?

Getting Ready

Sign Me Up!
Students sign up for weekly tasks in a community garden.

GOALS

- Students work cooperatively to plan and perform an act of kindness for the school or the larger community.
- Students reflect on their feelings as they make a positive difference through acts of kindness.

MATERIALS

- chart paper
- Mindful Action Planner sheet (p. 158)

CREATING THE OPTIMISTIC CLASSROOM

Brain-Inspired Instruction Neuroscience validates what teachers know instinctively: Model the type of behavior you wish to see in students. Hold yourself and students to the same high standards by:

- offering sincere and specific compliments to students and colleagues regularly.
- greeting students with a smile and address each by name.
- following up with students when they mention important events in their lives.
- making time to discuss students' concerns, as a group or one-on-one.
- acknowledging the kindnesses you see among students—publicly, if appropriate.

Students will try to live up to what you expect of them, especially if they see you making the same effort.

Digging In
Working toward an altruistic
goal together builds camaraderie
among students.

MINDUP Warm-Up

Taking Action Practice

Talk to students about the different spheres of influence they might have. Begin with school, and work outward to neighborhood, town or city, state, and so on. Represent this expanding system of cause and effect on the board or chart paper by making a dot and ringing it with concentric circles of increasing size. Label them with all the spheres of influence that you generate, ending with the world or possibly the universe!

Challenge students to come up with an example for each level of influence. Some ideas might overlap more than one sphere. For example, students might start an organic garden at the school or in the neighborhood. Strive to have at least one idea for each ring you labeled.

Discuss: Discuss the advantages of putting your focus in different places.

Leading the Lesson

A Strategy for Service

Engage

Explore

What to Do

Invite students to reflect on having an impact in the different spheres of influence they identified in the warm-up. Relate that exercise to this lesson's idea of choosing an action to take.

Ask students to brainstorm some mindful acts of kindness that would make a difference in these different spheres—at school, in the community, or in a distant place.

- You are all noticing more ways you can help out through acts of kindness. Let's think of how we can make a powerful impact for another group or cause in our school or neighborhood or even across the world.

- What are some problems nearby or far away that you've heard about lately? In which sphere would you locate these problems? What actions might help?

Make a class list of concerns and actions. Guide students toward projects you will be able to help them manage, such as a clothing collection for flood victims or a neighborhood park cleanup. Narrow the list and have the class vote on one.

Involve students in planning for the group's chosen act of kindness.

Inviting student input, make a general to-do list or fill in the Mindful Action Planner activity sheet. Then have students sign up for tasks such as

- researching charities
- making a detailed event schedule
- writing invitations or announcements
- listing and finding materials needed
- communicating with people who may be willing and able to help

Alternatively, you may want to tackle each task together as a class.

Show students on a calendar how to work backward from the tentative date of the event to set due dates. Allow time for students to work together to complete the tasks. Revisit the to-do list and any other checklists or reminders students have developed as you prepare for the mindful action event.

Why It's Important

Brainstorming helps students become invested in the group action. As you generate the list, adjust the amount of information and guidance you provide, based on student responses. You might gather students' general ideas (e.g., hunger, natural disasters) and then browse charitable organizations online by category to find several in which students may be interested.

Planning uses important executive function skills that require use of the prefrontal cortex—predicting, evaluating, backward planning, delegating, and so on. Offer to help students with planning and organization. Doing different tasks over the course of several days in short, focused periods will help. Post a calendar with key dates and tasks marked, as a visual reminder. Tasks can be color coded.

From the Research

A comprehensive mission for schools is to educate students to be knowledgeable, responsible, socially skilled, healthy, caring, and contributing citizens. (Greenberg et al., 2003)

Reflect

After students have completed the service they planned, invite them to share their experiences and reactions.

- What were you able to accomplish?

- What problems did you encounter and how did you solve them?

- How did you feel about your mindful act of service before, during, after?

- Would you like to perform more acts of service in the future? Explain.

Ask students to connect their experiences to what they've learned about their brains.

- How could taking mindful action be a healthy workout for your brain?

Students realize that they can accomplish great things for themselves and others by giving service. They get an optimism boost and learn life skills while solving problems and improving others' lives.

Students will learn that during mindful actions our amygdala calms down, our RAS collects information, our PFC makes decisions, our mirror neurons help us empathize, and our hippocampus stores the memory!

MINDUP In the Real World

Career Connection

One for one—that's not only the philosophy behind TOMS shoes, founded by Blake Mycoskie, but also the business model. For every pair of shoes this innovative company sells, it donates a new pair to a child in need. So when you buy a pair of TOMS shoes, you're not just buying for yourself, you're also putting shoes on the feet of a child without. Why shoes? Because in developing countries many diseases are soil-transmitted—they penetrate the skin through bare feet. Also, shoes protect feet from cuts and sores and enable children to go to school.

Discuss: Select several companies that make favorite products you buy. How could these companies implement the practice of "one for one" in a way that would help others?

Once a Day

Consider the way teaching can be a "one for one" service. How can you create situations where your teaching gets absorbed by students and then passed along to others in the school (e.g., buddy teaching with a younger group of students)?

Connecting to the Curriculum

Taking mindful action supports students' connection to their own learning process and to the content areas and literature.

Journal Writing

Encourage your students to reflect on what they've learned about taking mindful action and to record questions to explore at another time. They may also enjoy responding to these prompts:

- Make a list of the top five problems you think need to be addressed in this country and any ideas you have about solving them. Then find the address of your U.S. representatives and use your notes to write a letter stating your priorities and ideas.

- Think of a local problem that needs solving. Sketch an idea for a charitable organization that could help. What actions could be taken? How much money would have to be raised?

- Create a poster for your school to promote volunteering. Why should people get involved helping their neighbors and community? How can you persuade them to do so?

- Cast yourself in the role of good citizen of the universe. What kind of mindful action could you take that would affect such a large sphere? Express your ideas in a diagram or cartoon.

the Optimistic™ classroom journal

SCIENCE
Don't Trash the Planet

What to Do
Explain that everyone can be kinder to the whole planet every day by being mindful of the amount of waste thrown away. Discuss with students where waste often ends up—landfills, incinerators, the deep ocean. Be sure students understand that the garbage trucks may move it someplace else, but it doesn't go away, at least not until it decomposes after many years. Have students research how long it takes before common objects decompose.

What to Say
I'd like each of you to keep track of anything you throw away for a single day. It will be a one-day trash diary. Together, we'll analyze your lists to find the most common items. Finally, we'll break into groups to research how long it takes these things to decompose. We can put our findings on a wall chart. Seeing the impact of our trash might inspire us to reuse, recycle, and reduce consumption.

Why It's Important
This activity combines awareness of our impact on the environment with a commitment to taking mindful action. The trash that gets hauled away ends up in our land, air, or water, and it stays there for many years. It's likely that future students will look back on our current waste management systems with the same shock we get when we see people toss trash out a car window.

SOCIAL STUDIES
United We Stand

What to Do
Challenge students to take a virtual tour of the United Nations http://cyberschoolbus.un.org/. Direct them to the UN Introduction, under Resources, so they can learn about the history of the organization. Then give them time to explore the site. Ask them to report back on something they learned about how this organization functions in the world.

What to Say
After reviewing some issues that the United Nations is tackling, what did you learn? Some of the problems are very serious and upsetting. How might you use your new knowledge in a way that leads to mindful action, rather than feeling overwhelmed? List students' ideas and encourage them to follow up.

Why It's Important
This activity can connect students to the history of the twentieth century, as well as to current events taking place around the world. Students can apply this new information to what they've learned about taking mindful action.

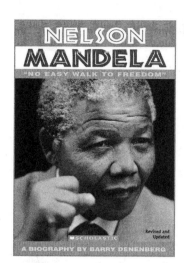

MATH
Analyze Dollars Spent

What to Do
One way for students to research charitable organizations is to find information about how they spend donated money. This information is usually included in an organization's prospectus or annual report. Often this information is available online. Pie charts are typically used to present a snapshot of how the organization allocates its funds. Introduce the word "development" as a synonym for fund-raising, as that is usually a major allocation.

What to Say
Let's make a list of some charitable organizations that you may know about and have some interest in: Habitat for Humanity, Meals on Wheels, United Way, CARE, Heifer International, and so on. Next, we'll pair up and choose a charity to research. See if you can find the pie chart that shows how they spend their money. Then, we'll compare them.

Why It's Important
Students can employ chart-reading skills in the interest of mindful action by researching popular charities to see which spend more of their dollars helping people. Students can use this information to select charities to support through individual or group effort. This type of research is also a good consumer-related life skill.

SOCIAL-EMOTIONAL LEARNING
Mindful Act of the Month

What to Do
Regularly celebrate students who take mindful action based on what they have learned in this lesson. Set up a place to post information about student efforts and results. Invite students to create a display of or report on their project.

What to Say
Let's not end mindful action with this lesson. Any students who continue to take mindful action should keep the class informed. The class will vote on the Mindful Act of the Month and the person who did the mindful act can create a wall display with pictures, notes, and artifacts or give a report.

Why It's Important
Encouraging students to remain dedicated to mindful actions will help keep many of the MindUP skills in focus—from mindful awareness to perspective taking to choosing optimism. It will expand students' understanding of the larger world and remind them that making positive changes really does make us happier and our world a better place.

Literature Link
Nelson Mandela: No Easy Walk to Freedom

by Barry Denenberg (2005). New York: Scholastic.

This biography of Nelson Mandela will introduce students to his struggle against the injustice of apartheid and demonstrate his enormous resolve despite long imprisonment.

This biography connects to mindful action or may resonate with other causes that have captured students' interest on the continent of Africa. Have students discuss the mindful decisions he made, and how he led others in the cause.

More Books to Share

Hoose, P. (1993). *It's Our World, Too: Young People Who Are Making a Difference.* New York: Farrar, Straus & Giroux.

Lewis, B. (1992) *Kids With Courage: True Stories About Young People Making a Difference.* Minneapolis, MN: Free Spirit.

Lewis, B. (2009). *The Kid's Guide to Service Projects:* Minneapolis, MN: Free Spririt.

the Optimistic classroom™ library

Brain Power!

Label each part of the brain and explain how it helps you.

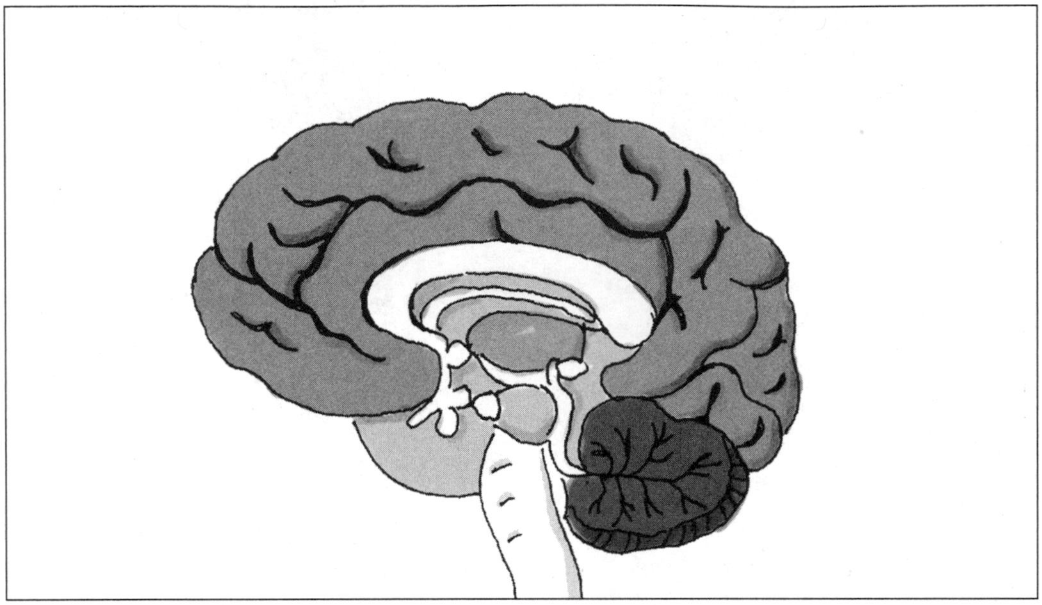

prefrontal cortex   **hippocampus**   **amygdala**

The prefrontal cortex _____

_____

_____.

The hippocampus _____

_____

_____.

The amygdala _____

_____

_____.

Name _____

Date _____

Mindful or Unmindful?

Mindful	Unmindful
Thinking about the weather and your schedule for the day as you get your clothes ready	Thinking about what you are going to say next when someone is speaking to you
Making small changes as you practice a new skill so that your performance gets better	Ignoring pain or other signals from your body that tell you that you're hungry or tired
Listening to a new song all the way through before deciding if you like it	Trying to do too many things at the same time, like walking and texting
Trying foods that are different from anything you've eaten before	Liking things because other people like them
Taking time to notice if someone around you needs some help or would like your attention	Daydreaming or "tuning out" to what is happening without really noticing and hearing things around you
Looking at someone's face when you're talking to them, to see how they are reacting to what you're saying	Not taking the time to notice whether other classmates may want to join your game or group

Name _____

Date _____

Audio Alert/Present Scent

Mindfully listen to the mystery sound or smell the mystery scent. Describe what you notice about it and the people, places, or things it reminds you of. Make a guess and then fill in the name of the sound or scent.

Details I Notice	What It Reminds Me of	My Guess	Actual Sound or Scent
1.			
2.			
3.			
4.			
5.			

Name _____

Date _____

Sensory Web

In the middle of the web, write the name of the object or specimen you're observing. Fill in as many sensory details as you notice to describe it.

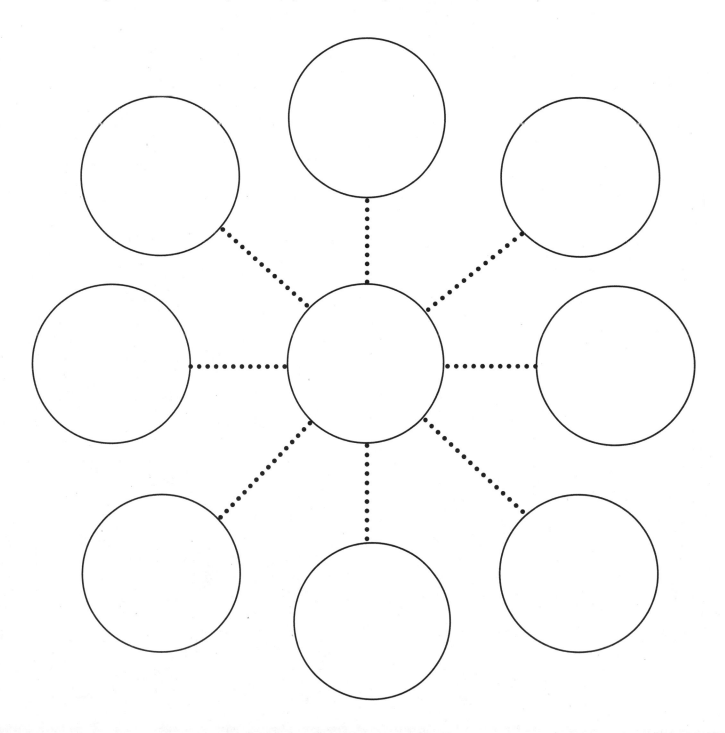

Name _____

Date _____

Character Perspectives

Examine the way a character reacts to events in a story in order to determine his or her perspective.

Title of Story: _____

Name of Character: _____

Describe a key event in the story.

_____

_____

What words, thoughts, and actions show the character's reaction to the event?

Words	Thoughts	Actions

What does this evidence reveal about the character's perspective?

_____

_____

Name _____

Date _____

Optimistic/Pessimistic/Unrealistic Thoughts

Think about a problem that you or someone you know has faced. In one sentence, describe the problem. Then fill in the thought bubbles to show an optimistic and a pessimistic reaction to the problem.

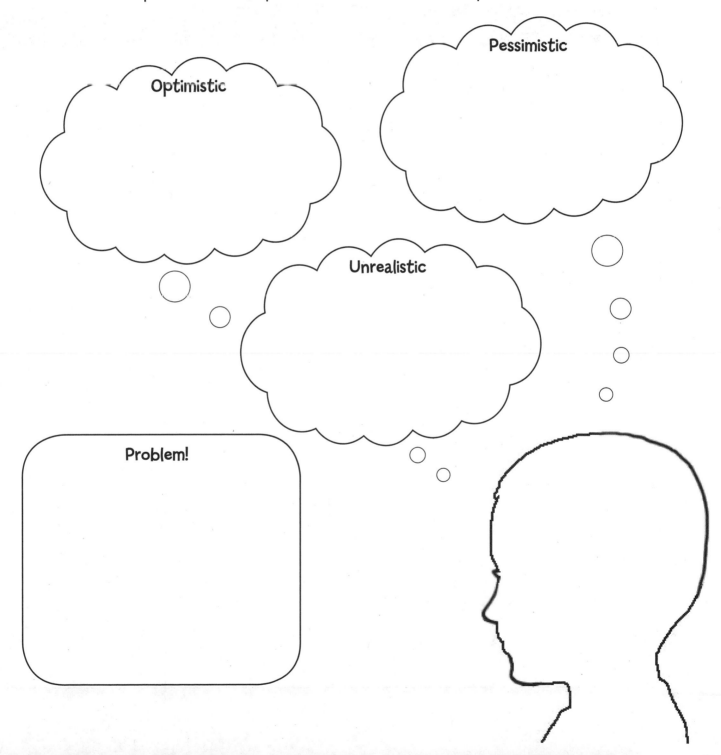

Optimistic

Pessimistic

Unrealistic

Problem!

Name _____

Date _____

Mindful Action Planner

Event _____   Event Date _____

Task	Materials We Need	Date to Finish	Who's in charge

Glossary

adrenal glands
organs located on the kidneys, responsible for releasing stress hormones such as cortisol and adrenaline (epinephrine)

amygdala
an almond-shaped structure which is a part of the limbic system that encodes emotional messages for long-term storage in the brain

brain stem
a brain part, comprising midbrain, pons, and medulla oblongata, which receives sensory input and monitors vital functions such as heartbeat, body temperature, and digestion. The RAS is located in the brain stem

Core Practice
deep belly breathing that relies on mindful, focused attention; it is recommended that the core practice be done three times each day for a few minutes—depending on the age of the student

cortisol (hydrocortisone)
a hormone produced by the adrenal gland in response to stress or to a low level of blood glucocorticoids, the primary functions of which are to increase blood sugar, suppress the immune system, and aid in fat, protein and carbohydrate metabolism

dopamine
a neurotransmitter that produces feelings of pleasure when released by the brain reward system; has multiple functions depending on where in the brain it acts

endorphin
a neurotransmitter with properties similar to opiates that are important for pain reduction and the creation of pleasant and euphoric feelings

epinephrine (adrenalin)
a hormone secreted by the adrenal glands

executive function
mental management that includes higher-order skills dependent upon the thinker's ability to reflect before reacting: evaluating information, organizing, focusing attention, prioritizing, planning, and problem solving

fight, flight, or freeze response
neurophysiological mechanism of the sympathetic nervous system in response to real or perceived threat

glutamate
the most common excitatory neurotransmitter in the brain

hippocampus
a brain structure that compares new learning to past learning and encodes information from working memory to long-term storage.

hypothalamus
a brain structure at the base of the limbic area that regulates body functions in response to internal and external stimuli, controls the pituitary

limbic system
the collection of cortical and subcortical structures, including amygdala and hippocampus, situated at the base of the cerebrum that control emotions, motivations, and other behaviors, and are important for memory functions.

mindful attention
focused awareness; purposeful, nonjudgmental attentiveness

mindfulness
state of being in touch with and aware of the present moment in a nonjudgmental way. Mindfulness is an approach used by mental health professionals as a kind of therapy that helps people suffering from difficulties such as anxiety and depression.

mirror neuron
a neuron that responds when one performs a certain action or when one observes the same action performed by another. Thus, the neuron "mirrors" the behavior of the other, as though the observer were performing the action

neural pathway
usually, a series of nerve bundles that connect relatively distant areas of the brain or nervous system

neuron
a nerve cell, which is a cell specialized for excitability and conductivity, composed of an axon, a soma, and dendrites. (All neurons have one soma and one axon; some neurons have many dendrites and others have none.)

neuroplasticity
the brain's lifelong ability to reorganize neural networks as a result of new or repeated experiences

neuroscience
an interdisciplinary science focused on the brain and nervous system and closely associated other disciplines such as psychology, mathematics, physics, philosophy, and medicine

neurotransmitter
one of many chemicals that transmit signals across a synaptic gap from one neuron to another.

norepinephrine
a neurotransmitter and a hormone that is part of the fight, flight, or freeze response. In the brain, norepinephrine acts as a neurotransmitter—usually excitatory, sometimes inhibitory—to regulate normal brain processes.

positive psychology
scientific study of the strengths and virtues that enable individuals and communities to thrive. (Understanding positive emotions entails the study of contentment with the past, happiness in the present, and hope for the future. Understanding positive individual traits consists of the study of the strengths and virtues, such as the capacity for love and work, courage, compassion, resilience, creativity, curiosity, integrity, self-knowledge, moderation, self-control, and wisdom. Understanding positive institutions entails the study of the strengths that foster better communities, such as justice, responsibility, civility, parenting, nurturance, work ethic, leadership, teamwork, purpose, and tolerance.)

prefrontal cortex
a part of the brain that dominates the frontal lobe, implicated in executive function, planning complex cognitive behavior, personality expression, decision-making and moderating correct social behavior and considered to be orchestration of thoughts and actions in accordance with internal goals.

reticular activating system (RAS)
a dense formation of neurons and fibers in the brain stem that controls major body functions and mediates various levels of brain response

social-emotional learning (SEL)
the process of developing the fundamental life skills needed to effectively and ethically handle ourselves, our relationships, and our work

synapse
the microscopic gap between the axon of one neuron and the dendrite of another, that serves to connect neurons. Synapses connect them functionally, not physically, enabling neurons to communicate by passing signals between them.

thalamus
receives and integrates all incoming sensory information, except smell, and directs it to other areas of the cortex for additional processing.

unmindfulness
lack of awareness; uncontrolled actions, emotions, or thoughts

Resource List

Allyn, P., Margolies, J. & McNalley, K. (2010). *The Great Eight: Management strategies for the reading and writing classroom.* New York: Scholastic.

Alston, L. (2007). *Why we teach: Learning, laughter, love, and the power to transform lives.* New York: Scholastic.

Ashby, C. R., Thanos, P. K., Katana, J. M., Michaelides, E. L., Gardner, C. A. & Heidbreder, N. D. (1999). The selective dopamine antagonist. *Pharmacology, Biochemistry and Behavior.*

Brown, K. W. & Ryan, R. M. (2003). The benefits of being present: Mindfulness and its role in psychological well-being. *Journal of Personality and Social Psychology*, 84(4), 822–848.

Caprara, G. V., Barbanelli, C., Pastorelli, C., Bandura, A. & Zimbardo, P. G. (2000). Prosocial foundations of children's academic achievement. *Psychological Science, 11*: 302–306.

Collaborative for Academic, Social, and Emotional Learning (CASEL). (2010). Retrieved from: http://www.casel.org/basics/skills.php.

Diamond, A. (2009). *SoundSeen: In the room with Adele Diamond.* NPR. November 19, 2009. Retrieved from: http://being.publicradio.org/programs/2009/learning-doing-being.

Durlak, J. A., Weissberg, R. P., Dymnicki, A. B., Taylor, R. D. & Schellinger, K. B. (2011). Enhancing students' social and emotional development promotes success in school: Results of a meta-analysis. *Child Development.*

Galvan, A., Hare, T., Parra, C., Penn, J., Voss, H., Glover, G. & Casey, B. (2006). Earlier development of the accumbens relative to orbitofrontal cortex might underlie risk-taking behavior in adolescents. *Journal of Neuroscience.* 26(25), 6885-6892.

Greenberg, M.T., Weissberg, R.P., Utne O'Brien, M., Zins, J.E., Fredericks, L., Resnik, H. & Elias, M.J. (2003). Enhancing school-based prevention and youth development through coordinated social, emotional, and academic learning. *American Psychologist, 58,* 466-474.

Greenland, S. K. (2010). *The Mindful Child: How to Help Your Kid Manage Stress and Become Happier, Kinder, and More Compassionate.* New York: Simon & Schuster, Inc.

Goleman, D. (2008). Emotional intelligence. Retrieved from: http://danielgoleman.info/topics/emotional-intelligence.

Iidaka, T., Anderson N., Kapur, S., Cabeza R. & Craik, F. (2000). The effect of divided attention on encoding and retrieval in episodic memory revealed by positron emission tomography. *Journal of Cognitive Neuroscience*, 12(2). 267–280.

Jensen, E. (2009). *Teaching with poverty in mind: What being poor does to kids' brains and what schools can do about it.* Alexandria, VA: ASCD.

Jensen, E. (2003). *Tools for engagement.* Thousand Oaks, CA.: Corwin Press.

Kann, L., Kinchen, S. A. Williams, B. I., Ross, J. G., Lowry, R., Grunbaum, J. A. & Kolbe, L. J. (2000). Youth risk behavior surveillance in United States, 1999. Centers for Disease Control MMWR Surveillance Summaries, 49(SS-5), 1–96.

Kato, N. & McEwen, B. (2003). Neuromechanisms of emotions and memory. *Neuroendocrinology*, 11, 03. 54–58.

Lutz, A., Dunne, J. D., & Davidson, R. J. (2007). Meditation and the neuroscience of consciousness: An introduction. In Zelazo, P., Moscovitch, M., & Thompson, E. (Eds.), *The Cambridge Handbook of Consciousness* (499–554). Cambridge, UK: Cambridge University Press.

McCullough, M. E., Kilpatrick, S. D., Emmons, R. A. & Larson, D. B. (2001). Is gratitude a moral affect? *Psychological Bulletin*, 127, 249–266.

Pascual-Leone, A. Amedi, A., Fregni, F. & Merabet, L. B. (2005). The plastic human brain cortext. *Annual Review of Neuroscience*, 28, 377-401.

Pawlak, R., Magarinos, A. M., Melchor, J., McEwen, B. & Strickland, S. (February 2003). Tissue plasminogen activator in the amygdala is critical for stress-induced anxiety-like behavior. *Nature Neuroscience*, 168–174.

Payton, J. Weissberg, R.P., Dulak, J.A., Dymnicki, A.B. Taylor, R.D., Schellinger, K.B. & Pachan, M. (2008). The positive impact of social and emotional learning for kindergarten to eighth-grade students. Findings from three scientific reviews. Chicago, IL: Collaborative for Academic, Social, and Emotional Learning. Retrieved from: www.casel.org or www.lpfch.org/sel.

Posner, M. I. & Patoine, B. (2009). How Arts Training Improves Attention and Cognition. The Dana Foundation. Available: http://www.dana.org/news/cerebrum/detail.aspx?id=23206.

Ratey, J. J. (2008). *Spark: The revolutionary new science of exercise and the brain.* New York: Little, Brown & Co.

Revising the rules of perception, retrieved from http://news.vanderbilt.edu/2010/07/binocularvisio, posted 7/29/10.

Schonert-Reichl, K. A., & Lawlor, M. S. (2010). The effects of a mindfulness-based education program on pre- and early adolescents' well-being and social and emotional competence. *Mindfulness, 1,* 137–151.

Schonert-Reichl, Kimberly A. (2008). Effectiveness of the Mindfulness Education (ME) Program: Research Summary, 2005-2008. Retrieved from: http://www.thehawnfoundation.org/.../2007/.../summary-of-the-effectiveness-of-the-me-program_april2009ksrfinal1.pdf.

Shadmehr, R. & Holcomb, H. (1997). Neural correlates of motor memory consolidation. *Science 277*: 821.

Tatum, A. (2009). *Reading for their life: Rebuilding the textual lineages of African-American adolescent males.* Portsmouth, NH: Heinemann

Wentzel, K. R. (1991). Social competence at school: Relation between social responsibility and academic achievement. *Review of Educational Research*, 61(1), 1–24.

Willis, J. (2006). *Research-based Strategies to Ignite Student Learning: Insights from a Neurologist and Classroom Teacher.* Danvers, MA: Association for Supervision and Curriculum Development.

Willis, J. (2008). *How Your Child Learns Best: Brain-Friendly Strategies You Can Use to Ignite Your Child's Learning and Increase School Success.* Naperville, IL: Sourcebooks.